Praise

Discovering Family Constellations therapy with Marine has been one of the most profound experiences of my healing path, allowing me to recognize and move on from the limits of inherited family patterns in a way that is beyond words. Marine is a gifted and compassionate facilitator, and reading about her own journey with Family Constellations is fascinating. I also love the practical exercises she has included throughout her book, which open the door to anybody invested in learning to understand and accept the unique family history that has brought them to this place in their personal evolution. **Ruby Warrington**, The Numinous

How can I express my gratitude to this lovely young woman, Marine, who is so intuitive and gifted. Each experience I have shared with her and others in Family Constellation work has been deeply powerful and transformative. She is present and right there with you, wherever you are in the moment, supporting you and guiding you. I am in my late 40's and have completed many years of healing and self-process work, but have been blown away by the powerful work I've done with her. I have uncovered old unconscious, limiting beliefs from my past that I had no idea were present. It literally has been life changing for me. Working with Marine, what has been hidden, is revealed. What has been buried, comes up to the light, in its own safe timing, to be witnessed and healed. The unknown becomes known. She holds the light of Love and creates such a Holy healing space, a space of integrity and understanding. She is a wonderfully safe guide to let into your life, to hear your story, to witness your pain, and to walk with you on your journey. Thank you Marine, for everything that you've done, and for everything that you will do. *Kathleen*

Congrats! You are on to something big! God's purpose for you is a great one and I feel so blessed to have been able to meet such an amazing woman. You're an inspiration. *Cristina Horta,* DISfunkshion Magazine

Greetings Marine, I've been reading your blogs on Herfuture and Google + and I think your work is amazing. You showed me it is possible to forgive and let love in. *Yolima*

Your energy and passion for what you believe oozes out of you and it is infectious. You are a really special person, a beautiful person. *Denise*

Family Constellations is an amazing tool that helps you let go of things you didn't even know you were carrying and Marine is a wonderfully intuitive facilitator. Give yourself this book! *John Moore* – Peace Through Oneness

The Movement

*An authentic method to reconcile with your roots
and live the life you're meant to*

Marine Sélénée

The Movement

An authentic method to reconcile with your roots and live
the life you're meant to

Copyright © 2015 Maluga, LLC

First Edition

ISBN: 978-0-692-57423-2

Maluga, LLC

www.marineselenee.com

Dedicated to all the soul caretakers

"There aren't any unhappy adults, only misunderstood children."
Marine Sélénée

Table of contents

Preface

Marine called me for an energy reading. As I remember, what I 'read' and strongly imprinted in my mind was the word 'integrity', which seemingly contradicted the deep secrets I could detect Marine was keeping; hermetically closed in her broken heart.

What I also envisioned that day via telephone, was the wealth of potential the young women was carrying: I just knew she could reach her authentic power and free the diamond hidden under the rough rock. It would require a long journey into the dark nights of the soul, but it could be done.

I felt guided to take the challenge and act as a bridge: I invited her to join my weekly meditation circle.

That following Wednesday, when exposed to her striking beauty and impressive presence, I was relieved I already 'knew' Marine's energy, or in other words her inner beauty and potential so I could not be deceived by her 'perfect girl' looks.

Her outer appearance was an easy distraction from her wounded soul and the deep sorrow that she was hiding under her ice queen disguise and cool attitude.

The rest is history... and how I became deeply honored to influence Marine's ability to re-establish her "orders of love". Our relationship has had its moments: Marine often mirrored a very young version of myself I spent many years to heal, but the deep bond we share has always prevailed. I'm proud to have been the catalyst to her introduction to the Laws of Attraction and then, later on, Family Constellations.

When Marine moved to New York, I encouraged her to train with my friend and mentor Suzi Tucker with whom I had just completed my own training. I knew Suzi would be the right fit for Marine to continue to open and bloom as the flowers Bert Hellinger alludes to when he talks about the many facilitators who find their way to the 'field' – and therefore benefit the process in showing their own creativity. Marine gives us a taste of this in her very first literary attempt.

Today, I have the privilege to preface Marine's first book. I marvel at the clarity with which she shares valuable information and offers tools to the growing community we witness in the United States and rest of the world. *The Movement* is the perfect guide to get familiarized with the approach; it also presents us with an original concept to look at the perpetual movement of life and demonstrates how a Constellation follows the never-ending movement of the Soul.

Easy to follow, Marine's map of Family Constellations will help many to understand how unconscious loyalties and entanglements they triggered can be healed by the "next chance child", that is the one in the next generation who will seek answers; if as Marine has done, one is willing to show courage and determination by stepping into the 'knowing field'.

Michelle Blechner

An Encounter

The first day of the rest of my life happened randomly over tea time with one of my favorite teachers, Michelle, a spiritual healer and "joyologist" as she likes to be called, and someone who I consider to be like a maternal grandma to me.

Michelle was incredibly excited about a new discovery she had made during a trip to New York, a method called Family Constellations.

Even though I couldn't entirely figure out what Family Constellations was or meant just yet, her enthusiasm for it was so infectious that she got my full attention. Unknowingly, I was magnetized to Family Constellations and I couldn't wait to experience it.

Later on, I would find that this day marked a turning point in my life.

A few weeks later, Michelle invited Natalie Berthold, a Family Constellations practitioner, to facilitate some workshops at her place in Miami.

There were only four people in the first workshop. It was a small and private group, which was perfect for me because I didn't know what to expect or how to act. I was very nervous but I have to say that the professionalism and serene behavior of Natalie, my facilitator, helped me greatly to trust her and the process.

Natalie asked what I wanted to work on. I said I wanted to attract the man of my life – and figure out why he was not here yet!

After asking a few more questions regarding my family history and dynamics, Natalie proposed I choose one person to represent my mother and another person to represent my father. Then, I was to place them both into what was being referred to as the "field."

While I explain what a constellation is in the following chapters, we can start thinking of how the Family Constellations process works through author and expert Joy Manné's insights. In her book, *Family Constellations: A Practical Guide to Uncovering the Origins of Family Conflict*, she notes that the client sets up a constellation by placing the chosen representatives (sometimes unknown to the client as to exactly who they 'represent') in certain spatial and directional positions that represent their relationship with each other. Placing the representatives is an intuitive process, done without thinking. After everyone is placed, the constellation emerges and an autonomous energy field is created. Then, the client and representatives work through their feelings in the field, as guided by the facilitator's observations and questions, until a resolution is reached – or it's clear that a resolution is not possible, which is a resolution in itself. What is a resolution? The feeling of being unburdened in relation to the issue and other representatives that was brought to light in the constellation field. "It brings peace and contentment to the family energy field," Manné states.

Going back to my first constellation, I don't remember who represented my 'mother' but Charlie, Michelle's husband, represented my 'father'. He was 90 at the time and had dementia. Charlie was one of the sweetest men I have ever met and even though he couldn't remember what happened just five minutes ago, he was an amazing representative.

When Charlie took his place as my father in the 'field', I was able to see my father's soul through his eyes. This deep connection was unexpected. How could Charlie represent my dad so well without even knowing him or his background? I was speechless. All my fears surrounding this new experience vanished immediately. In that moment, I was convinced something was happening for my greater good.

Charlie was the perfect example to show that when you step into the field as a representative (even with his dementia), you take on the energy, persona and true feelings of whoever you are meant to.

For me, this was first proof of Family Constellations' power. In the field, everyone is authentic – we speak and act out our true feelings rather than from our head or thoughts of what we 'should' do. We all benefit as soon as we connect with our heart, gut and intuition. We feel, experience, resist and then consent to 'what is' with love.

My first Family Constellations session lasted 40 minutes. The field showed me a truth I did not want to see – I was afraid of love – and therefore, my future partner. Family Constellations showed me that my heart was broken and I needed to repair it first.

Imagine my disappointment on one level, yet on another one, the immense relief to have a solution. I had to work on myself, love myself and heal my past... before I could find love. This solution was my responsibility alone and it gave me strength to keep going.

After that first time, I did many Family Constellations sessions for my own healing journey. Along the way, I started studying the Family Constellations approach so I could become a facilitator as well.

My life changed course. I no longer wanted to be in PR, I wanted to go back to my studies and embrace this new career, as an integrative coach, specializing in Family Constellations. My prior study and background in psychology helped prime me for this new path, which instantly felt empowering and meaningful. This is how I started dedicating my life to serve others.

For me, Family Constellations was an epiphany. All of the secrets and burdens that bothered me were finally revealed through love. In the field, I 'rebirthed'.

To summarize the Family Constellations approach, I would say that each family has a heritage that passes down from generation to generation. We share the same last name and sometimes even the first name as our family members or ancestors; as well as the same bloodline, roots, culture and stories. An invisible yarn links us all together and through this, we can feel things that we may have never even personally experienced. Let's call this invisible yarn our loyal, internal family memory.

Our negative behaviors and situations are often entangled with our family system dynamics that have not yet been recognized. If we stay in these underlying entanglements, they will move into the next generation.

Family Constellations is a way to break this chain of blind behavior.

Family Constellations enables us to open our eyes to this secret or unknown pattern at work in our family. With this new awareness and perspective, we can free ourselves from entanglements we may have with current and previous family members – and find new ways to navigate. We will learn why we repeat certain negative, antagonistic behaviors. We will release negative patterns. We will analyze any issues blocking our way. We will cry. We will smile. We will feel oppressed and experience feelings we don't want to face for the last time. Then, we will experience new feelings that lead us to a new, beautiful and safe place. We will breathe again. We will trust again. We will love again. We will believe in ourselves again. Our ancestors have our back throughout this entire challenging journey. We will never be alone in the process. Remember, "The essential is invisible to the eyes," as Antoine de St Exupery expressed. Our ancestors are here, even though we can't see them.

Family Constellations will bring love back into our life, mind and body. Then, it is up to us to nurture this newfound love and sense of self. It's a commitment, not a miracle remedy.

My wish is that one day; we will all experience fulfillment within. This means we finally integrate the lesson that the past is the past – and more importantly, that our story from the past does not define who we are. Our 'story' can mean holding onto those negative thoughts, behaviors, or events we experienced to justify our current behaviors, addictions and why we 'can't' take responsibility for our lives. For example, the story could be "I can't get close to anyone because my mom never showed me love or how to do it". Or "I can't make money in my career because my parents never had enough money, so I don't know how or I feel guilty [that is, for being successful or outshining parents]". Another story could be "I'm aggressive and dominant towards men because my father treated my mother like nothing, so I take revenge for her honor". These stories are often unconscious and ones we aren't aware of.

We are the only one who can define ourselves. Whatever happened to us before – we must mourn it, accept it and then keep living our life to the fullest. Let's become the person we want to be and tell ourselves what we are capable of doing. We are in charge of our life, our destiny and can choose the life we want to live.

This breakthrough will be a tremendous moment. It will be the beginning of something new – a 'rebirth' – and I urge us all to embrace it.

Ultimately, Family Constellations is a process of rebirthing. A rebirth of love, truth and acceptance.

Family Constellations has changed my life.

While I believe the best way to truly feel the impact and power of Family Constellations is to directly experience a constellation, there is much to learn from studying Bert Hellinger, the founder of Family Constellations, and his observations treating families and individuals for more than 50 years with this approach.

I have included a list of recommended books and resources in the appendix for those who are interested to learn more about Family Constellations.

Marine Sélénée

« If there is a book you really want to read but it hasn't been written yet, then you must write it.»
Toni Morrison

Introduction:
Life is a Collaboration of Ups & Downs

When I was younger, I spent a lot of time with my grandparents during family vacations in a town called Carnac in Brittany, France, famous for its dolmens.

Their home had a beautiful, blue porch swing on the patio, which was my own little heaven on earth.

Perched on this porch, buoyed by its gentle rocking movements, I clocked up many precious memories – tea time with my dolls, breakfasts with grandma and naps with grandpa, to name a few. These fond memories helped me through challenging times later on.

If I felt unhappy, all I had to do was jump on my swing and instantly, my sadness was gone! The rhythm of the porch swing had this magical power to instantly calm me. It was a pleasant reminder of when my mother cradled me.

The porch was my safe place. When I started doing therapy, I used this place as a visual "comfort blanket" for my mind.

Life itself is a movement that goes up and down. When we think we have it all figured out, our life will 'move' again, placing us in front of a new obstacle or opportunity that requires our full attention. Even though it is for our best, sometimes we can feel challenged, afraid, angry, lost or even resistant towards this new experience. We might want to give up, walk away from this new 'stage' or let our ego take over. Yet we can overcome a new challenge and create something great from it.

If we are still skeptical, at this point, I would invite us to reflect on our past for a few minutes – what have we already achieved in our life?

After this short retrospection, please, let's congratulate ourselves on our own unique journey so far.

I have been through many challenges and opportunities and all of them, positive and negative, made me who I am today. These experiences allowed me to discover and become familiar with my own life expression.

I met extraordinary people who gave me great tools and advice to keep going on my healing journey or 'movement', as I like to say.

My mother was my first wonderful person. She always supported me and tried her best. My mom was my strength and hope when I only saw darkness.

Then, I crossed the path of Emmanuelle Barré, a specialist in Eye Movement Desensitization and Reprocessing (EMDR)*.

EMDR is a comprehensive, integrative psychotherapy approach that combines elements of various psychotherapy treatments – psychodynamic, cognitive behavioral, interpersonal, experiential, and body-centered therapies – in a structured way for maximum effect.

We worked together for three years. Emmanuelle allowed me to reveal my true feelings and speak my truth. She was incredible. I will always feel a special connection with her.

After I moved to Miami, I met Michelle Blechner. She became my teacher on my spiritual journey. She introduced me to Abraham Hicks, the Laws of Attraction, meditation and Family Constellations. At first, Michelle made my head spin! I didn't understand what she was talking about. Finally, one day, I woke up and all her teachings made sense to me. She is the one who taught me to love myself as I am.

I will always remember when Michelle introduced me to Family Constellations. She was so excited about it! She sung its praises: "Marine, you have to try [it]! It's terrific! I was speechless! I couldn't believe it!"

For Michelle, Family Constellations was the missing link. For me, it was the beginning of a new movement, an empowering movement that set up a tremendous life change.

Michelle was right. I was speechless after my first constellation. It blew my mind. In one session, I understood so many things. I realized that this method was the final touch for my healing journey. I was ready to accept my past and my different experiences. Family Constellations helped me follow through. It was intense. I did many constellations. I cried a lot but every time, it was followed by the same beautiful feeling: serenity. I released tons of bullshit, false beliefs, issues and burdens. Step by step, I realigned my own movement to be true to myself. I dropped my heavy weights. I liberated myself! Such a powerful sense of freedom!

Then one day, I felt the call to become a Family Constellations facilitator. I followed my intuition and completed the Guided Learning course with Suzi Tucker at the Bert Hellinger Institute in New York City, USA, where I started spreading the word about this tremendous approach.

I have facilitated numerous constellations now and every time, it's a personal revelation. I feel so honored to be part of the clients' process. When they get their resolution, it's always an illuminating moment where even I feel the love that is coming back into their life. I love witnessing their movement. I love seeing their enlightened face, thanks to the release of so many burdens.

I am truly passionate about Family Constellations. I have read widely to deepen my knowledge of this practice and found that two key ideas form the crux of Bert Hellinger's overall philosophy on Family Constellations: firstly, 'the profound movement of bringing love back into the family system', and secondly, 'that if there is one central key in life, it is Love'.

In my book, I have added all the 'ingredients' I gathered during my healing journey to create a multi-layered recipe (a hint of this and a dash of that!); blending various techniques with Family Constellations theory at the core. I hope it will give us the desire to go back into our past one more time in order to move forward into our present, as well as find great ideas that we can personalize for our own healing journey.

Because as soon as we know where we come from and entirely accept it, we can move onto our life's path in full swing.

It's only a small adjustment, but this 'only' could make a huge difference in our life. Grab this chance to deeply embrace the feeling of completion and achievement through knowing our roots.

I believe everyone deserves to live a happy life and embrace their purpose with excitement and presence. Remember that life is supposed to be Fun!

My book is divided into 33 chapters to resemble the 33 vertebrae that make up our spine. Our brain resides in our spine, which is why the spine can become twisted, arched or imprisoned to support itself and the brain's directives. Like a tree's stump, we need our spine to grow up straight while staying grounded in our world.

After reading my book, metaphorically, the spine will be complete...and therefore holistically, the brain that aligns with it. I truly love this image of having a beautiful, noble and strong spine as a strong and noble family tree.

One last thing – writing this book in English was a challenge! Three extraordinary women helped and supported me during the long yet exciting process.

Alison Savary, Suzi Tucker and Sophie Coleman; thank you all so much for your trust, patience and great insights. Without you all, this exciting new adventure wouldn't have been the same. I bow to each one of you.

I wish you a delightful discovery of Family Constellations; maybe one day we will even share the same field.

"When the field enlightens your shadows, don't be afraid or run away from them. Be assured that behind your shadows, there is your Love, waiting for you. Reach out for this Love and bring it back into your life. This is what I call 'the Movement'. The Movement of Love."

Marine Sélénée

* For more information about EMDR, please refer to the reading list in the appendix.

"A little girl with a yellow dog, holding a red balloon was walking into the streets…"

To my parents, I could not have had better parents than you. I love you.

The Beginning

This first chapter provides the 'backbone' to my healing journey and why I dedicated my life to Family Constellations. Every following chapter will then highlight the most common patterns we see in Family Constellations.

I was born into a wealthy, wonderful family. While we had our share of infidelity, alcoholism, depression, gambling and so on, these issues never seemed to perturb our gleaming smiles. We looked 'picture perfect' on the outside but behind this, the story was different. The truth is, we are good soldiers in my family. We take care of our 'afflicted' members and that always engendered respect by our neighbors, colleagues and friends. This is how my family system worked until I stuck my nose in.

Did I break this beautiful image? Perhaps. I was simply trying to reorder things with love. I wanted to release the secrets and pain that my beautiful family of soldiers had been carrying for a long time. As my teacher Suzi Tucker said, "every child is a next best chance" to realign the family system. I guess I took my mission very seriously.

Why did I have this urge? Let's say that I wanted to understand where all the suffering and burdens came from. The beautiful picture of my family didn't fool me. I felt uneasy sometimes and for me, this was a clue that there was a chink in my family system. I was determined to find and repair it.

At first, my main concern was my father's side of the family, which seemed to be in great disorder. The pieces of the puzzle were all over the place and I wanted to understand why. Despite the information I gleaned during adolescence, it was not enough for me. My knowledge of his family was cruelly lacking for me. This hindered my ability to reconstruct my family story. I was determined to get answers. Why was he so uncomfortable with his mother? Why did my grandfather disappear? Why was my father so nostalgic and hypersensitive? Why was my father not a 'normal' father? Why didn't my grandmother love me but so admired my brother?

I completed the pieces of my family puzzle over 15 years, helped largely by Family Constellations. When I placed the last piece, I felt whole and complete. I didn't get all of the answers but I found everything I needed to know, which allowed me to make peace with where I came from.

When I was introduced to Family Constellations, I saw it as a way to heal my family and myself, as well as a means to reconnect with my father. My first Family Constellation blew me away. I worked on relationship issues, convinced my problems with men only related to my father. I was wrong. My mother and lineage of women in my family also played an important role in my love life. Unconsciously of course, they were still very present and invisible ghosts for me at that time.

For me, the most magical, impactful part of the field was how it revealed the truth with respect and love. There was no judgment or blame in the field, only love. In this sudden, new harmony, I experienced profound relief; automatically followed by the thought "I want to be part of this."

I fell in love with Family Constellations and had a strong desire to become a facilitator firmly planted inside me. My three main teachers: Mark Wolynn, Michelle Blechner and Suzi Tucker. I would also like to honor all of the people I have worked with as a participant in the field – for their different interpretations of me and my family, which were always on point. Thanks to them, I was able to 'clean up' my story! Suzi Tucker was my mentor in my learning process and helped guide me from where I was, to where I needed to go. I truly admire this woman for her vulnerability, where her strength resides. I was captivated by her facility to conduct a constellation. She would float into the field instead of merely enter.

My respect for Suzi grew even stronger on May 10th, 2014. Finally, after many different therapies, Suzi was able to liberate my destructive pain. I am convinced that without all of the other therapists and healers who took care of me before however, that I wouldn't have been able to face what I had to face during this constellation.

When I registered for her Guided Learning course, I told Suzi my story. I felt it was important she knew, so that I didn't have to talk about it again in front of a group.

A few workshops happened before I was willing to work on my issue. After approaching her, Suzi responded to my request with "I was waiting for you." A few minutes later, we were setting up my constellation.

I picked someone to represent me. Then, she asked one man to enter the field. With my representative, the issue appeared right away. After five minutes, Suzi asked if I was ready to take my place. I was. In front of this guy, all of my suffering rose to the surface. It was violent, cruel, and fierce; I could barely breathe and stand. Suzi asked all the women in the group to stand behind me. Still, it was not enough for me to stand up. My knees were weak. I could feel they wanted to split. I was crying and screaming that I needed my mom. This pain was consuming and burning my entire self, while simultaneously I trusted the process. I guess at this exact moment, Suzi understood that I clearly needed my mother and she went into my field to represent her. I will always remember the strength of this tiny woman holding me like my mother would have done. For the first time in my life, I was facing my traumatic event with a strong person, my mother, holding me. It allowed me to release my tears, my pain, my rage and my anger. I was freeing myself from this devil and it felt so empowering. It took me 15 minutes or maybe more to start breathing again, slowly and calmly. Suzi never stopped holding me with this particular, fierce strength.

Finally, my pain ended.

It took me 15 years to free my body and mind from being sexually abused at the age of 13. It was my secret, my scar, my heavy weight. I never told anyone about it. When I was around 15, I shared a few clues with my parents; however I also didn't want them to know. After all, this had taken place on the trip that was meant to build a strong future for me: it was an exceptional gift from my parents to have the opportunity to become bilingual. It was true love. How could I ruin it?

After the sexual abuse happened, I had a blackout and kept pretending I was a regular teenager. I was pretty good at it. I had lovers but never good ones. By choosing the wrong man every time, I kept on punishing myself. In my mind, I deserved it.

After my last important relationship (and marriage) ended, I made the decision to fall back in love only when I was entirely healed. I was a young woman, exhausted by love and men. I was fed up repeating the same behaviors and attracting violent, cheating or alcoholic partners. I finally chose myself, on April 10th, 2009, to be exact.

After a few years of intense healing, I found myself again and truly became "I".

For this reason, today, I am able to talk and write about my experiences. I made peace with that part of my story. This occurrence does not define me. I am the one who defines me and this understanding clearly improved and empowered my life.

Would I have become a facilitator and an integrative coach if I have not lived my past as it was meant to be? I don't think so. I think the role of our past is to polish and prepare both our present and future. All of those experiences brought me here today to New York. I am reopening my heart more and more to love, as well making peace with my body. Sometimes, I tumble or feel dizzy; nevertheless I know now that in my vulnerability resides my true strength, which is my true identity.

How can we get over a rape or another traumatic event?

Our past events do not define us. We are born to shine.

I want to say that whatever happened, it was not our fault. Mourn this period and move on. Somebody else needs us. Find this person. Be someone. Chest up my girl. Chest up my boy. Let's be proud of ourselves. We deserve everything and more again.

Life goes on, influenced by our environment as much as aspects of our seen and unseen character. I have no idea how I survived. I only know that my little girl Marine was determined to live. My little girl had a bigger, better picture for me and she put her feet in mine, which gave me support to keep on walking, even when I was crawling.

I believe it doesn't matter how we make it; what truly matters is our willpower to move beyond failure and our determination to nurture the feeling that we have the right to live fully.

My inner child showed me the way to Family Constellations. The adult became one of its students and facilitators.

For the past three years now, I have dedicated my life to becoming a better integrative coach and facilitator every day.

With an open heart and strong desire to be fully authentic with my words, I dedicate my book to all of us who want to heal and live life to the fullest. My book is here to show us ways to bring trust, faith and love back.

Our choice of way doesn't matter, as long as we enjoy the ride.

As many healers say: "healing is a journey, not a destination."

With love,
Marine Sélénée

*"In remembering the truth of where we came from,
we become more open to the truth of who we are."*
Marianne Williamson

Imprint

The first thing we learn in Family Constellations is the importance of acknowledging, respecting and accepting our family as it is. This approach encourages us to accept and respect our past, instead of disowning or romanticizing it.

As my teacher Suzi Tucker says, "You can run or merge with it, it will be the same thing. You are still not looking toward the life to come because what has past still transfixes you."

Family Constellations is a way to give us total freedom to choose the life we want to live and to follow our destiny, without being held back by our lineage.

We belong to our family. I would also add that we belong to our community, culture, country and the countries of our ancestors. When we honor this full package given to us by our previous family generations, we experience a steady and powerful strength.

In Family Constellations, an image or role play is set up to illustrate that Dad is behind us on our right side and Mom is behind us on our left side. Both of them are followed by their own parents, grandparents and ancestors behind them in the same pattern. This is an influential image that can imprint and affect our life for the best.

I was born in France. Even though my parents are both French, on my father's side, my origins are a nicely charged melting pot of three different countries: Prussia, Germany and Argentina.

I was raised by my parents and mainly by my mother's side of the family, who were very present in my life.

At my parent's wedding, my dad only had a few guests including just one family member: his mom. The rest were all from my mother's side.

I knew my father's mother but we were not very close.

For as long as I can remember, I was always clueless and full of questions about my paternal lineage. I always felt that something was missing in my life.

My father, who I would describe as a mysterious and secretive person, would sometimes tell us things about his childhood, but not much. Those rare moments when he did talk about his past were very solemn and a privilege for me. When he shared his stories, I felt more accepted and trusted by him. I felt that I was part of his life. But, still those little pieces of 'his story' were not enough for me.

I was ready to solve the mystery of my father's lineage on my own; for me, it was like the board game Cluedo, asking more and more questions to try and solve the enigma!

I was convinced that one day, I would bring my family together and finally my dad would be at peace. I was wrong. I understood it a few years ago that the past is the past and we can't do anything about it, except accept it as it is, without any resentment or pain.

We don't have enough energy to live in the present and still try to resolve our past. If we keep going back to our past, we will probably not be as happy as we could be on this Earth

Unfortunately, my parents got divorced when I was 23 and my quest of solving the enigma brutally ended. My dad decided to cut himself off from my brother and I then.

I was upset and angry towards him, albeit in a passive way. Then, this anger moved towards my mother and finally to myself. What did I do wrong?

A lot of invasive thoughts and questions swirled in my mind, an intense roundabout that seemed to have no end. I wanted to understand. I wanted to find answers. I wanted to see my father. I was lost. I was confused about our sense of family belonging. Weren't we supposed to be always together? No matter what happened...

The truth is – family blood doesn't give us an automatic, unlimited connection. We can share the same blood with our family members, yet our family can be toxic for our well-being sometimes, so we need to detach ourselves from this bond with respect and find a new current with other people. It's not always easy and pleasant to go through this process and shift onto another vibration, but it can be a crucial step to take in order to have a happier life.

In all that confusion and endless questions without answers, a miracle happened.

In the end, my parents' divorce sparked me to find my purpose and how I could serve the world. Even though it took me a few years to understand the blessing in their divorce, thanks to that time full of foggy, blurry situations, I gained the distance I needed to understand and make peace with my father, giving birth to a bright new dawn. Then after eight years of silence, I finally reconnected in a beautiful, unpredictable way with my father.

My father did not have an easy start in life. His dad abandoned him and my father's dream of becoming a pilot never came true.

His life seemed to repeat this pattern of rejection until he met my mom. His wife was his rock, a chance to live instead of merely surviving. My parents formed this rare couple where no words were needed to see that true love existed between them. How could I imagine that one day they were going to divorce?

In my mind, my parent's separation was impossible, even though sometimes during my childhood I asked mom to divorce him because he had been mean and severe with me. As a child, this could be quite common I'm sure!

From my new perspective as a facilitator now, I can see why the divorce was inevitable in a way. There was a missing piece in the family system and life will always find a new path to fill this hole and heal it.

Of course, in leaving us, my father ended up doing to his children exactly what had been done to him. He repeated the pattern of his first, most profound rejection of abandonment by his father, carrying this forward in the system from inheritance to legacy.

A few months after the divorce, it was my turn to leave my country and therefore, my family. My place was not in France anymore and I had this urge to move on and close this chapter of my life. I wanted to break free from my family. I couldn't handle the new love of my mom, the suffering of my brother and, as the icing on the cake, I had married and it was a disastrous relationship! So I ran away. I needed to breathe! I hit rock bottom. The good news, I later learned, is that once we hit rock bottom, up is the next logical direction! It may take days, months or even years but we will make it. I know this because I made it!

For a long time, I oscillated between desperation and joy. One day, I was a mess; the next, a 'tidy' one. I was fighting for my present life, trying to build something from all the ruins of my past. It was impossible to manage. Everything was frustrating. I was looking for my place and role in my family and society. Thankfully, on this dark road, I met great people and discovered so many new teachings, two especially that imprinted my recovery the most – the Law of Attraction and Family Constellations.

Finally, these teachings gave me a concrete solution. I was able to see the light at the end of the tunnel. It took a while to peel away the different layers of my suffering, but every new tiptoe forward brought me closer to my rebirth.

The fireworks and final touch for my rebirth happened in New York. The move from Miami helped me to quickly finish my healing work. I built strong foundations to ground me in my new life, allowing me to reach my dreams and expand my career.

For this reason, I chose to serve others. I believe my past and all of my experiences are actually my best 'business card' to be a legitimate, authentic life coach and healer, which is very important for me.

Those years focused on my own personal healing reinforced my sense of belonging to my family. My healing showed me where I came from, so that I could move forward into my present moment. It taught me that nothing lasts, neither the good nor the bad. Everything can become love in a minute; it's a matter of choice and claiming another perspective.

All of us are part of a Family Constellation. Every member of our family can be seen as a star. With his or her own means, every person illuminates something. They share their story. The story may be clumsy, violent, disappointing, funny, hilarious, loving, tender, dramatic, but be reassured that every act and behavior comes from only one place: the place of love.

Honor and bow to each member of the family.

When we will feel depressed, angry, sad and so on, lean on the family. They will support us. They will send us enough love to overcome whatever the issue is. The only behavior that allows us to honor our ancestors in all their power is trust. Know that they are strong enough to take care of us. We don't need to turn our back to our present to check if they are still there. They are. The best way to feel their presence is to close our eyes and let them surround us.

Can you feel this wave of power and love?
Then, let's be ready to follow our path. All of this work and recognition leads to an absolute truth that everything and everyone is perfectly placed.

Everything is in order.

Let's keep going on our task of healing -- and always keep going again.

We are protected. We are loved. We are trusted.

Affirmations

Affirmations can be a useful support through important life changes.

I have included affirmations that are specifically designed to help with the issues raised in each chapter. Choose the affirmations that resonate with you the most and leave the rest.

We will start by recognizing and accepting your place in your family system:

I belong to my family system.

I only know myself through you.

I am your daughter/son. I am your sister/brother. I am your mother/father.

If you feel any discomfort, tension or resentment, you can create other affirmations or stop for a moment.

Family Tree

I have included a short exercise or reflection at the end of each chapter to help our self-discovery, as well as clarify situations that we may not have fully understood when they first happened.

If you don't feel comfortable with my suggestions, you can always adjust the exercise or find another one. Trust your inner voice, your best guidance.

For our first exercise, draw your family tree. On the tree, note the dates of birth and death of family members, as well as any important or major events – war, abortion, marriage, divorce, murder, children given away, suicides, dramatic financial losses or gains, slavery, insanity, and so forth.

When you are done, take a look at your family tree and look for any patterns or repetitions – the same date of birth or death of family members, repeated disorders, any traumatic events that occurred at a similar age, or exclusions from the family through homosexuality, disabilities, or being a single parent.

Circle the event that is the most traumatic, or strikes you the most when you look at it. Then circle the event that gives you the most strength.

Let your different thoughts and insights come into your mind and pass through. Look at your family tree with love. One by one, thank each member for being part of your family system.

How do you feel?

Sheltering the Inner Child

Over the generations, children are recruited by the family system to bring the family back into balance. A child can be seen as another try to resolve anything that was not acknowledged in the past family generations. Some children can be elected by the family soul to reclaim excluded members, for example. This process, while unconscious, is real in the family system.

Even though it would be so much easier for us to live fully when our parents carry their own guilt and when they bear the consequences of their acts, so we no longer have the compulsive urge to atone or compensate for them; most of the time, it doesn't flow like this. We are loyal to our parents.

This is why as a child; we will do everything to heal our mother, while we simultaneously chase the thwarted dreams of our father. We work on both their behalves, whether we know it or not.

If our mother or father is depressed, we might become a funny clown or depressed as well. If our father has committed suicide, we will probably commit suicide, either literally or in leading a deadened life. If our mother had three abortions, we might abort as well or not desire to have children at all. Again, these are unconscious movements that might create resentment or anger towards them.

By acting like our parents; it's our inner child who is still trying to fix its family. Because, every child is the "next best chance for the world" as Suzi Tucker, one of my teachers, likes to say, and so for the family, their purpose is to bring back the order of love into the family system. Unfortunately, it's a heavy weight to carry.

In the field, we are able to drop this heavy weight and release any unconscious patterns that hold us to this early designated mission. Plus, this work will deeply heal our inner child.

We have to remember that as an adult, our role is to serve and protect our inner child. If our inner child is still sad, angry, disappointed or frustrated, we will be as well. All of our frustrations, pains, worries, and doubts come from our past. By healing our inner child, we can drop our pain and finally be free.

One last point: normally, our parents want the best for us. If this is not the case in our family, the only thing we can do is to accept them as they are. Honor them and love them as they are. They did the best they could. Now, it's time to enjoy our life without this feeling of guilt that we couldn't heal our parents. No one can heal his or her parents! The only person we can heal is ourselves. This is an important gift that we make to our family as well. Because by healing ourselves, we offer a space of healing for the next generations.

Accepting our parents as they were and are is not just a good idea – our life may depend on it.

Affirmations

I follow my own path, not the fate of others.

I will do something great with my life.

I will let go today. I will bring myself back to the present. I don't need to make up stories in my head.

Family Heritage

What is your family heritage? Your grandmother's joy? Your father's anxiety? What is there to pass on? What is there to keep? What is there to get rid of it? What is there to release?

Make three lists:
1. Positive and negative things that you have picked up from your family generations, past and present.
2. What do you want to keep and pass on?
3. What do you want to release?

Order & Disorder

In Family Constellations, we take great care to put things in order.

The most frequent family disorder issue I have witnessed in Family Constellations – as a facilitator, representative or observer – is when the child takes care of his mother/father and becomes the adult, while the adult becomes the child. This reversed role situation is very common and can be resolved during one or several constellations.

We proceed by placing the parents of the client behind him or her, with the father on the right side and mother on the left side. The client's parents will then be followed by their own parents and so forth.

This is a beautiful picture to keep in mind – to see and feel our ancestors behind us.

I have experienced this type of constellation, where I saw my lineage behind me and believe me, it was a deep, emotional resolution that released so much in my life.

There is logic in the family system, so when things are back in order from generation to generation, we can finally be in the present moment instead of the past. By reorganizing the past, we bring a new image of the family order into the present. From that new image, a new energy will emerge that will diffuse relief between every generation. And this is what we call a resolution.

The first important tenant of healing raised in Family Constellations is the importance of finding the right distance between ourselves and our mom, and ourselves and our dad. Secondly, even though we fit differently into our family, we all have a role to play. We are all important and deserve to be recognized.

For this reason, it is vital to reset a new order to guarantee a continuous flow of prosperity, happiness and love towards our own journey.

When I work with my clients to rehabilitate any missing order, I love giving this example that one of my best friends shared with me.

This little tale shows how things have their own order in the system and the importance of acknowledging this hierarchy within the order. This results in an endless, steady and prosperous flow.

« You have a vase. You place different sized stones and sand in it. If you start with the sand, you won't have enough space to fit the different stones. You have to start with a strong foundation, which is represented by the bigger stones. Then, the smaller ones, which are supported by the strong base. And at the end, you put the sand in that easily finds a way to perfectly blend with the strong and steady foundation. The sand is not blocking the foundation or other stones. The sand is adapting itself to this system. And this is what life is…. »

When we have a strong and steady base, we can move on into our destiny and not pay attention to whatever has happened in our family past. The role of our ancestors is to have our back; this is the only appropriate manner to honor them. Then we can feel the lovely presence of our parents behind us, they have our back as well. And here we are, full of strength, leading our generation that will one day, give birth to a new one.

This is the cycle and purpose of life and our assignment is this: to live our life as it has been gifted and aligned to us.

Affirmations

What I think is missing on the outside is within me waiting to be found.

By reordering things in me, I bring love back into my present.

I am whole. I am enough. I am complete.

Create Order

Create your own vase; it will be a nice reminder that as long as our family order is maintained, everyone will be able to move on and be fully present in their life.

I did mine by using various buttons and sequins in different colors and sizes. But you can use anything you are drawn to – stones, shells, sand, soil or marbles. It's your vase, your order and your creation.

Enjoy the craft!

Continuity & Departure

During one of my Guided Learning classes with Suzi Tucker, we talked about stepparents, half siblings and stepsiblings. She asked us to raise our hands if we had stepparents. In this instant, I became very confused! I didn't know where to stand.

My parents divorced when I was 23, so they had already raised me into adulthood by that stage and taught me everything I needed to know. The job was done.

My mother remarried. From my perspective, her new husband was only a part of the new family system they set up together, which I had nothing to do with as I already had my own family system.

Yet I still felt guilty about my hesitation. I wanted to know if my behavior toward him was okay or if I had to make some adjustments.

I explained my situation to Suzi. Her answer was crystal clear and it helped me to accept him as he was and not want to change him anymore. I was finally free to step back into my first position, as my mother's daughter.

Suzi's words brought peace back into my heart.

"He is not your stepfather. He is your mom's partner. She looks at you with this man at her side. Find a way to open your heart to his heart so that you include him in your private sphere, with healthy boundaries."

I truly loved this image of finding a way to open my heart. This simple approach worked perfectly for me and brought me peace regarding my mother's new relationship.

Freedom is to just be who we want to be. I think we can apply this delightful teaching to other relationships and situations that happened and will happen in our life. We will meet people who we won't appreciate. However, with the power of an open heart and full acceptance of them as they are, things will always flow.

A divorce is a difficult and intense period. No one is ready to experience the end of a marriage. Yet because a start depends on a finish, this finish has to be done properly.

If parents divorce and remarry after 18, this generally means we won't have a stepparent in the everyday sense. We are already on our own path. And if we think of the stepparent in this way, we might be disrupting our family system by having them replace our biological mother/father figure.

Is our father absent from our life? Are we close to our mother? Let's take a look at our family system to see where the missing link is. Then we could ask ourselves, "Am I displacing my feelings?" "Am I looking to heal my relationship with my father with the new husband of my mother?"

If the answer is yes, I recommend that we make peace with our inner father/mother in a family constellation or another approach. This allows us to move on in our own personal love life.

When I say inner father/mother, I am talking about the presence in our body, mind and spirit of our parents. I am talking about the connection we have with them on a deeper and mystical level. It's a connection that we make through our womb. This connection is instinctive when we first understand that those two people are our parents and they gave us life.

Our body is liberated when we make peace with our inner parents. We will only carry the best from them at this point, and release the burdens we carried for them previously.

Divorce is another dynamic if it happens before 18 years of age. Everything can work out well or become "The War of the Roses".

As Bert Hellinger said, "Divorce is a matter between the parents and it's not the children's business."

I concur.

Unfortunately, most often the adults' storm sweeps up the children. The parents ask them to choose their camp, either overtly or covertly. They are put in the middle of this war and expected to be a counselor or a mediator, which is inappropriate and devastating.

Here, Suzi Tucker advises: "If the parents include each other even as they withdraw from one another, the children have an easier transition."

The family system will stay the same in a divorce. While a divorce spells the end of a love story between the parents, the love for the children should not be questioned. The family system will always provide a safe platform if the parents remain together inside the children, that is, when parents remain active in their roles as a mother and a father and keep their children out of divorce. They are and will always be 'together' for their children as a couple of parents' couple. Then regarding their couple as a man and woman in marriage, it is their own business and has to stay like that.

Ultimately: a child must not interfere in the parent's affairs. Parents have to bear their own choices. We must stand in our role – as the child – and focus on our own future, so we don't live in theirs.

Furthermore, Suzi Tucker provides an interesting thought: "Rejecting the other parent is rejecting the other parent inside the child."

I agree with her. If we don't accept our ex-wife or ex-husband with love and respect, how can we imagine that we can properly love and accept our children as they are? That child has the ingredients of both the mother and father!

Let's take a look at the stepparent's side, which is not easy either. He or she arrives in an already established family system. With the new partner, this person will set up a new and different system with other rules and beliefs.

How can we find the accurate balance between the two family systems that now have to live together?

Why not see a stepparent as a positive new energy that can illuminate a new world?

As long as the stepparent doesn't try to be 'more' than the biological parent, which is a potentially threatening behavior to the fragile equilibrium that is trying to get stronger, it will work.

Like the children, the stepparent needs to stay in his place, respecting and honoring the biological father or mother. This includes not saying any negative words or criticisms about him or her.

When it comes to younger children, parents need to pay attention to any behaviors that try to oppose the adult's authority. This can seem funny or harmless at the beginning because the children think they might get more gifts or attention from their parents, but they will soon experience more drama and misunderstandings by impacting the parent's roles.

They have to accept the decision of the divorce and recognize that it was an adult decision.

They can't free themselves from their parents by thinking they know more than them. Their parents did the best they could and love them no matter what decisions they made. Don't stand between them; receive the best of them.

Through my Family Constellations experiences, when everyone stays in their place, there is a serene and established flow. Everything may not be perfect but at least when the family system is in order, aligned with everyone's roles, this lays the foundation for the present.

Affirmations

I simplify things in my life today.

My parent's relationship as a couple is not my business

As I respect my parents' decisions, I respect myself.

A Start Depends on a Finish

For this topic, my suggestion is a reflection on any new starts that you had to take or new ones coming.

In your journal, write down any thoughts that come to mind on new starts – such as taking on a new apartment, a new school, culture, or even a new bedroom can seem like a challenge at first.

You might think: why do /did I have to accept this situation when it wasn't my choice? Why do I have to open my heart to this stranger? Why do I have to find a way to appropriate and integrate this new chapter that has opened?

Everything is in movement. Nothing lasts forever. All lives evolve in an endless movement.

Every time a new circumstance occurs, the best thing to do is to stand before it with your own truth, beliefs and love. Find a way in your shadows that will lead you to a new place full of light.

Adapt by taking the best from this new person or situation and tweaking it as you wish.

"In Family Constellations, we notice how crucial anniversaries can be. The great impact the age we were when we experienced a trauma can have in one of our descendants, or the way our body reacts when we reach the age of a member of our system with whom we are entangled. Each one of those strange occurrences often seen as 'coincidence' by a less trained eye becomes obvious when you start to understand the way the spirit mind moves."
Bert Hellinger

Bonding

Every family dynamic has key dates connected to it. It could be the same date of birth or a specific period where there is a tendency for the same events to reoccur. We need to pay attention to these dates so we can illuminate and release the pattern.

As we discovered in the first chapter's family tree exercise, a family tree can help us discern various dates of birth and death of our ancestors, as well as any significant dates through the different generations. We can ask our grandparents, parents or other family members questions about particular events in their past – such as war, miscarriages, suicides, weddings, abortions or addictions.

Family Constellations asserts that we can produce an impact over seven generations: three before us, our current generation, and three after us. In fact, when we work on the emotional level, we can create shifts in many places. So, are we ready to break the spell?

For my family, I made a few connections regarding things that occurred at similar ages. Here are a few examples that I resolved through the help of the field.

A lot of tragedy happened in my family around the age of 13, especially on my father's side.

My grandmother lost her father. My grandfather had to stay in France during World War II for four years because his parents, who were in Argentina, were not able to bring him home. My brother went to boarding school. And I was sexually abused in London at the age of 13.

So as we can see, there are definitely abandonment issues and trauma around this age for several members of the family, me included. Could we have avoided this pattern? I think so and perhaps any member of my family was ready to break this particular curse, however they were probably not aware there was anything wrong at that age in the first place to acknowledge and bring to light in the family system, which is what Family Constellations endeavors to do.

Another interesting period for my family occurred in the early 20s age period. When my mother was 23, she wanted to move to the United States but because she was already married, she stayed in Paris and kept on going with her life. And guess what? At 23, I married, moved to the United States and then left my husband a few months later.

My behavior can be seen as a blind, loyal atonement for my mother. Because my mother was not able to pursue her dream, I unconsciously did what she wanted to do, so then my mission could be seen as a 'success' from my inner child's perception.

I atoned for her because she did not follow her wish and thus, the order was reinstated in our family dynamic through fulfilling an unacknowledged wish.

As we can see, the soul of a family will always create an event or find a way to close an unfinished cycle.

Another key date in my family was when my dear maternal grandmother passed away on July 16th at 1am. I am convinced that even though she had Alzheimer's disease, she was aware of not dying on the day of my birthday, which is July 15th. Otherwise, my date of birth would have been entangled with the death of my beloved grandmother.

One of the men in my family was born on the same day as his grandfather. He shared the same issues of sex and alcohol addiction with his grandfather. They also shared many other similarities, including having two marriages, a lot of lovers and dramas happening around the same age.

Another outstanding fact was when my grandfather turned 80, he shared a few of his secrets with us. I guess when we become older, our tongue loosens up!

The secret he told us was that before his wife (my maternal grandmother), he was with another woman and they had a son together. Their son passed away at the age of six months. Unfortunately, my grandfather had already left her and never knew about his son until the age of 79 when he met his first love again. She told him that she knew that one day, they would see each other again and decided to wait for him. She never got married. The astonishing thing is that when my mother was a little girl, she used to ask her mother "Where is my brother?" Of course, my grandmother always told her that she was her first child so that she never had an older brother. I guess the little girl could feel the presence of her half-brother. This is a remarkable example of the unconscious, invisible connection that we all have with our family system.

I will always remember this special moment. It was Christmas in 2012 and while the disclosure was a gift for us, the relief on my grandfather's face told us that it was a gift for him too.

Indeed, when a secret is revealed by the person or people involved with it, it can powerfully impact the family system's well-being. Family members may make connections between the confession and their behaviors and thoughts. This can lead to a deep shift and release many burdens and misunderstandings.

However, sometimes we might know that something happened but never know the exact story or details surrounding the secret. Even though this can cause frustration, our 'emergency exit' is to accept the secret as a fact and the silence in which it lives. More often, it is better to recognize a secret or an exclusion with love and respect, without knowing its full story. Endlessly seeking out the details can keep us in the past, in the sphere of the life that happened before us.

Besides the pattern of sharing a major event around the same age or date of birth with a family member, giving a child the same name as a deceased family member could also have an 'entangled' impact on their life, that is a connected fate in some way. Indeed, giving someone the same name can be linked with remaining in or repeating the same fate (death at a similar age for example), if we don't acknowledge the person who died early.

While often this is seen as a noble act, as far as I am concerned, we have to deal with so many things from our lineage already – that ideally, we don't need to carry another aspect through the name that can be avoided!

A newborn is a new life, beginning and cycle. Let's give him or her a chance to take the best part of their lineage and create something great from it with a fresh start.

If you are in this situation, I recommend you learn about this part of your heritage. Recognize any tragic events that occurred, then separate yourself with love from any entanglements that you might have with the passed family member or child.

It's a wonderful adventure to truly know where we came from. My only recommendation is that when that discovery process is no longer enjoyable, please let it be. This means our work is done and that we know everything we are meant to know.

It's always important to know when to start and when to finish.

Affirmations

**I can share the same date of birth [or name] of my ….
However, I don't share his/her fate.**

I have my own fate.

I belong to my family by living my own destiny.

Me in My Place

If your grandparents are still alive, I invite you to ask them if they would like to share something from their past with you. Give them space to share what they want. If you get a "no", respect their decision without insisting. Communicate with respect and without judgment, as you would like others to relate to you. This is a crucial key for the family dynamic's well-being.

I hope this exercise will help you to get new insights about your decisions and the choices that you have made. This way of looking into the family soul can expand your heart and ease anxiety. Plus, it will allow you to feel more grounded in your place and role.

"One of the foundational principles in constellations is that excluding a person who belongs to the system creates suffering and that restoring his or her rightful place brings relief." Daniel Booth Cohen

Flow Back

Absent people hold tremendous energy in the family system. They cause anxiety and fear, even though it's not deliberate. This is why it is so important to recognize any loss or 'absent people' in the family, be it through abortion, miscarriage, childbirth, suicide, murder or otherwise.

In Family Constellations, we can see when we are dealing with a missing person who has not yet been recognized. Usually, all of the participants are looking down. Who are they looking at? Who is missing?

Generally when a person is entangled with a deceased person, he or she unconsciously takes over the fate of this absent member of the family and lives it out. So if we behave dangerously or have many accidents, we could take a look at previous family generations to see if anyone died in a dramatic way or at a young age. We might resonate with the event or pattern immediately.

I had the honor to be part of several constellations where people were lying down and needed to be recognized by their family system.

For example, a woman was afraid to give birth because one of her great grandmothers passed away while giving birth.

Another woman who experienced feelings of extreme rage had been entangled in the fate of her father, who had murdered her grandfather. A man who attempted to kill himself five times was entangled with a cousin who had committed suicide. And another man who was in a number of car accidents was actually entangled with his father who had been in a serious car accident.

Plus, I have witnessed that when abortions are not recognized, this is dangerous for the family system's equilibrium, and especially for the living siblings.

In all of these constellations, many tears were flowing. In all, the energy was very intense and painful at first, however after a few minutes; we experienced a new flow of serenity and release in the room. It was breathtaking, beautiful and a respectful ceremony towards this person who was waiting to be recognized and accepted as a member of the family system.

When the dead have their place, they are peaceful and they are finally experienced as a positive energy. Therefore, the flow of abundance, joy and love will come back into all the different generations.

By taking care of our dead, we will take care of our next generation.

Affirmations

I will hold onto the gift of life you have given me as long as I may. Only when my time has come will I follow you. Please give me your blessings if I continue to live my life.

I honor your fate.

I see you and I will give you a place in my heart.

<u>Ceremony</u>

Look at your family tree and check the dates of deaths or unknown dates. These are probably the people for whom you will create the ceremonies. A recognition ceremony can be done with a letter, a balloon, a fire, or some other form of ceremony to signify a farewell.

If you want to address a letter to the absent or deceased family member, you can start with "I acknowledge you and I am letting you go…" Then, trust your heart and write whatever you want to share with this person.

For the "balloon or fire ceremony", you can say, "I honor your fate. I recognize you as a member of my family and I give you a place in my heart." Then again, let your heart speak for you.

The only important thing is to feel very deeply inside of you: "I am doing this ceremony for you now; you can finally be at peace."

Two Roots for One Seed

In Family Constellations, we talk a lot about the diverse dynamics and entanglements between past and present, and why it is so important to heal those two periods of time and accept them as they are. As I said, healing is about finding the right distance between us and our parents. However, there is another interesting character in this field to consider: our roots.

What do we know about our roots? From which country are our great grandparents or even grandparents? Do we know the story of our family's journeys?

The silent impact that our roots can have on our behaviors is a big surprise.

For example, Austrians and Germans who carry many issues and burdens are often related to war and Nazism. Many have to confront issues that involve victim stories or guilt for being alive.

In France, abortion has had a great influence. As one of the first countries to permit abortion, many French women in the 1960s and 1970s had one or more abortions.

Abortion is one of our fundamental rights. It's not my role to judge women who had one or who will. Accepting and honoring others as they are and their choices is one of my teachings and strong beliefs; we see the importance of accepting others in the Family Constellations field as well. It's their choice and so their freedom to be.

Having an abortion is a very delicate and painful moment for any woman. I have done many Family Constellations on this pattern. Every time, tears are present when we recognize this pregnancy and baby as it was, so the client can finally make peace with herself and her aborted baby.

And every time, the person representing the aborted child is always full of love for their mother. Because, this child had a mission and when they feel recognized by their mother, they are happy for her.

A woman can unconsciously carry the pain of an abortion through sabotaging her life until the end, while the child will be always at peace because they were always aware of their mission.

There is always a meaning in being pregnant, and it is our role to understand its significance. Family Constellations is a beautiful way to make peace with that event.

In Italy, the "mama' is very present in the family. Consequently, it's hard for Italian men to become independent from women's emotions because they have been connected and immersed in the emotions of their mother. They need their "mama" so they will always look for the perfect representation of their mother in another woman. This request can present a problem. Our lover is not here to be the twin of one of our parents. Until we recognize that idea, our love life will probably look more like a nightmare than a fairy tale.

In the Netherlands and Norway, there are a lot of 'sailor stories', that is, many fathers were absent through their occupation. So because the father did not fulfill the father's role, a lot of sons embraced this status. The masculine serves the feminine. When a woman takes care of her family by herself, the masculine is suppressed and not respected anymore. Boys who come from such families may display a distorted form of masculine behavior because their sex is seen as useless by the women/mothers. Often these men develop an addiction to someone or something – religion, sex, drugs – as a way of agreeing to their supposedly "useless" roles.

In the United States, the impact of immigration is a common story in many families. America has always been seen as a "New World", where people can pursue the 'American dream' cliché. Many people left their country and immigrated to the US during and after WWII, or other wars. For those family generations who were born after this immigration, it can be difficult for them to find their place sometimes, whether intentional or not. More often, they think they have to 'pay a price' for their life. They might bear the guilt of their ancestors who survived a war or other conflict. Here, a constellation could help give the guilt back to their ancestors in order to lift the burden; allowing them to move forward without feeling ashamed about living well.

In Brazil, the displacement or integration of indigenous people could be an issue. These natives sometimes have difficulty finding their place and role in the new society where there is no more authentic, strong value for them or their culture. Their family and culture always lived in perfect symbiosis with nature. The new culture, technology and habits can be foreign to them and their ingrained ancestral way of life. There's a huge gap between the two worlds and a clear loss of their way of life. Often, they lose their mind or commit suicide because they are not able to face this unknown world.

In several countries in Africa, there are patterns of rape, slavery and forced marriage. It can be devastating to the women's lineage, as they have to somehow make peace with men despite these feats. They carry a lot with them while also being brave and strong. These women live a beautiful act of resilience.

Last but not least, when one country has been invaded by another and the invading country's culture takes over, men can't find their place in society anymore. So the resulting pattern may be alcoholism or even violence towards women. There is an unconscious, rigid belief that because they couldn't protect their country from the enemy, they lose their masculinity. Metaphorically they have been emasculated. At the same time, women in these countries become strong while being upset with their men. It's a complex, connected system of false beliefs that we have to realign with the order of love.

As we see, it's important to know about our family but also the history of our roots – our culture and our country at large. By having a bigger picture of our family tree, we will better understand our entire family dynamic.

Affirmations

I am grounded.

By knowing the history of my country, I can be a messenger for the next generation.

I accept the blessings of my country's past, the challenges and the pain, and will carry those blessings with me.

Digging

You know where you came from but are you aware of your country's history? If not, time to improve your knowledge. Go to the library, buy books on your country and talk with elderly people who could tell you some very interesting stories. It's important to know your country's history so you can share it with your own kids, as the history of your country is their history too, as well as with others. Don't forget, your mission is to take care of your generation in order to prepare for the following ones.

The Mother

My first birthday far away from my family was at the age of 24. My mom sent me a birthday card with a watercolor picture of Montmartre. On it, she wrote a note telling me to never forget my roots, where I came from and who loves me. She finished her note with a few lyrics from the song "N'Oubliez Jamais" ["Never Forget"] by Joe Cocker.

Lovingly enough, my mom used to dance to the same classic songs like these while my papa played them.

I remember she always turned on the radio as soon as she went into the kitchen. Many of my best memories with my mom happened in that room. Everything in the world seemed right while cooking, dancing, singing, laughing, reading our horoscopes, understanding each other and embracing our time together.

In the kitchen, I shared all of my thoughts, dreams, desires, doubts and fears with my mother. Every time, she always found the best words to calm me down. Every little thing she did was magic for me. She was my super-heroine, always smiling and loving life for what it is. Her endless love and optimism towards me kept me alive.

In Family Constellations, the mother is always the first person that we look at. Even though we ask general questions concerning the relationship that the client has with his parents, the mother has a "bigger" role, for the only reason that she is the one who gives birth, the one who carries us for nine months. She is the one who risks her own life to bring forth another one.

Maybe, our mother was not the mother that we were expecting and our relationship with her is tough, filled with many misunderstandings and unsaid things. The essential thing to note is that one day she gave us the gift of life. Through us, she believed in the power of life and love.

And for that alone, our role is to honor and respect our mother as she is. She did the best she could with her own doubts, fears and past. That's not easy, I think we have to be completely faithful about life and jump out of our comfort zone knowing that no matter what we do, we will always make clumsy mistakes and be criticized. Taking care of another human is probably the most difficult and unrewarding task on one level.

If we embrace our role as a mother happily, our children will feel it. For sure, they will always have complaints and make some remarks about our absence or the way we raised them, but as we already know, this special and invisible bond between a mother and his child is unbreakable.

Through the relationship with my mother, I understand this last point. I have been unfair with my mom and not only once! I was only focusing on my own emotions and perceptions, pretending that because she was the adult and my mother, she had to understand my way of thinking; she had to take care of me as I wanted and she had to love me as I expected. I was so wrong.

Before being my mother, she was a little girl, a teenager and then an adult. She was not only my mother, she was at first a woman with multiple facets that gave birth to the kind of mom she was. Not the opposite. And when I understood that my mom was not perfect, I allowed her to make mistakes. I talked with her to understand her own way and this is something that I really enjoyed and still do.

Playing together when we were younger was nice but I love having a beautiful mother-daughter relationship as an adult now. I can talk with her about many subjects. We always have something to say. It's relaxing. It feels safe.

I am aware she did the best she could in her own way. Her own way and manners perfectly adapted for the young child that I was and the adult that I am now.

I chose her as she chose me and since then, my attention towards her reflects my choice – a good choice of love.

Sometimes, the love for our mother keeps us alive. My love for her permitted me to push back my own limits, to expand my perception of my world, to believe in tomorrow, to love again and to have unconditional faith about my talents and my own person.

Metaphorically and physically, she made me. I am a part of her and she is a part of me.

When we fully accept our mother, we fully accept ourselves. The same thing goes for our father. We are our parents and we can't change this truth.

So, let's stop fighting against our parents and our love for them. Let's lay down our anger, disappointment and pain towards them and just look at them as they are -,a woman and a man – who one day were also two young children and teenagers. They learned, they fell, they made mistakes, but despite their past and maybe a relationship with their own parents that was not ideal, they believed in their capacity to create another life through their love. They made a commitment together that they could become parents, for better or for worse.

So please, let them dance and play their own music with profound respect. Give them their places standing behind us – our father on our right side and our mother on our left side – and feel their love and support. No matter what has happened between us, they will always be here for us and if not physically, be reassured that we will be always connected energetically.

Mom and Dad, thank you for the gift of life. Through my brother and I, the music that you created together will keep on growing forever.

Affirmations

Thank you mom for the gift of life.

You are my mother; I am your daughter (or son)

You did the best you could. I will take it from here.

The Gift of Life

Write a letter to your mom with your best memories of her and send it to her. This will be a fully expressed gift of love without any expectations from her.

The Father

In Family Constellations, we often witness that the father struggles to find his place in the new relationship between his wife and their newborn. Normally the mother has already created a bond with this new life, this new child during the nine months of pregnancy. She's already established a dialog with her future daughter/son. For the father, it's another story.

Even though, he can be very present during the pregnancy period, he cannot fully understand what's happening. For sure, he is aware of his new role coming but until the baby is born, he may have difficulty perceiving himself as a father. He needs to see, touch, cuddle and feed the baby on his own. He needs to create his own bond with his child. Unfortunately, the mother (sometimes) does not give her husband a chance to bond right away with their new born. And, because of this behavior, the father figure steps aside and loses his trust regarding his capacity to be a good father.

A wife needs to allow her husband to become a father, make room for him and trust him. A man needs to be comforted in his capacity as a new father and guide for his family.

It's very important to create this balance. The woman gives birth. The man sets up a safe world by being the guide to it.

The father also plays an important role in our future relationships. If a daughter has a serene, respectful relationship with her father, she has a grand chance of creating beautiful relationships with future partners. For a son, the relationship with his father impacts how he respects women and the world; how he stands as a man, confident in his presence and authenticity.

A father is as essential as a mother. He has a different role than the mother but it is equally important. A mother and a father create an equilibrium within the child and when this balance is respected, the child will become a confident and happy adult.

Remember that to create a life, there needs to be two people and this extends to raising a child in most cases ideally, there needs to be two.

For the first 20 years of my life, I had a very symbiotic relationship with my mother. For a while, my father could not exist in this duo. Now, I can see that it was not healthy for all of us and thanks to my different healings; I finally have an equal relationship with both of my parents. Everyone has a place and this makes me feel more grounded and strong.

The father can also represent our feelings, behaviors and patterns towards love and other significant one on one relationships, business included.

What was I seeking through all of the men I have encountered? Maybe a little bit of my father. They were different in their flaws but all similar in their sufferings. They were broken. They were like my father, with fewer secrets and less of my father's presence that I wanted. They were a chance to understand my father better. They were lost and confused about my expectations. I wanted them to forgive my abandonment – the repeating pattern of my father - and save me from my shadows like superheroes. I wanted them to be passionately in love with me, while I remained close and far away from them simultaneously. I wanted them to be different than they were. For these reasons, none of my relationships were entirely filled with respect, love, communication and peace. They were filled instead with destructive passion, lies, infidelity, violence, and drugs. All of them were filled with fear. We were both already wrecks individually, so together we lived in a dangerous bubble of shared denial.

I thought love gave up on me, but what if I was wrong? What if I actually gave up on love and rejected love because I didn't want to deal with the pain of it anymore? My abuse experience at 13 years old - where I lost my innocence, dreams and future fairy tale – fed into this attitude to love as well.

I wanted to be the 'beauty', saved by the beast. I met a lot of beasts but none of them saved me. They were proud of my beauty but clueless about me. I am aware of my love failures. I played my role. I didn't want to be loved. I wanted to be rejected and excluded. I wanted to be brutalized. After all, if I thought my father couldn't love me, why would another man?

For ten years, I sabotaged all of my relationships. I wanted to feel the pain to feel alive. I wanted my father to save me. I wanted him to tell me how to act with men. I wanted him to tell me that I was beautiful and he was proud of me. I wanted him to look at me. I wanted so many things from my father that I did not get in the way I expected. However, today, I am fine with this statement. Today, I understand and accept my father as he is. I realized that my resentment towards him was only widening the gap between me and all men. I kept paying the same price.

Will I ever heal from my father's absence? To figure it out, I need to continue on my path. I need to feel love and give love again. I need to trust. I need to open my heart. I need to respect men.

Men are the guides of this world, while women carry life. Women give birth. Men lead our steps. When we respect their fate, their entanglements, their doubts, their fears, we accept them and so love will grow. The beauty of love lies in self-surrender, in the vulnerability of understanding that love is both tenuous and enduring. The uncertainty creates the urgency to love deeper and stronger.

The game of love can be vibrant and painful, all at the same time. Is it worth it? Yes. Men serve women as women serve men. It's an exchange. It's the pure essence of our roles.

I am thankful to all the men in my past: while our clumsy attempts at love didn't work for long, it worked for the time of our relationship. They made me grow and become a woman. Thanks to all of them, I surrendered my own limits. I discovered myself in our break-ups.

I have no regrets about any of the partners I had. We were meant to share something together. We were soul mates for a portion of the journey.

I believe a soul mate is someone who is like a newsflash for ourselves; they show us something that's missing. . This person will leave a mark in our life and play his or her part - bringing that missing piece into our life. A soul mate is only one piece of our puzzle, it could be the last piece and we won't know until we live with him or her. A soul mate also has a piece of us. It's a gift of self to them. It might appear irrational and unreal, but this person will help us to know ourselves better. And one day, for sure, we will meet our last soul mate. He or she will be complete as we are and together we will create another puzzle.

Let's remember that 'The One' is not here to complete us. He or she is here to enlighten and empower us.

This is what real love is, right?

Affirmations

I am ready for love.

I respect men.

My man serves me as I serve him OR My woman serves me as I serve her.

The Gift of Life

Write a letter to your dad with your best memories of him and send it to him. This will be a fully expressed gift of love without any expectations from him.

Note from the author:

In 2013, after a lot of work on my relationship with my father through Family Constellations, I had the urge to write him a letter. I was still uncertain about the possibility of ever reconciling with my father. However, I wanted closure. I wanted a sense of relief because I was finally able to understand why my father abandoned us. Or, to be more precise, I finally understood that it was not my fault. So I wrote him a letter, outlining my hopes and love for our relationship, which otherwise always seemed to get lost in misunderstandings.

Three years after, in 2015, my father and I reunited face to face in New York, completing the endless movement of Family Constellations.

The four days we spent together were full of peace and acceptance. We did not talk about the past; we only focused on the present moment and this new chance to create a balanced relationship.

I was just a daughter with her father, which felt very grounding and good.

Did this meeting finally happen thanks to Family Constellations? I believe it's a combination of a few things. In the end, the only thing that matters is that my father is back at his place, where he always belongs.

Intimacy

Sexuality, as I am going to refer to it in this chapter, means sexual expression between consenting adults.

Sexuality is a gift. A gift of love and deep, meaningful harmony between two people, who decide to create a deeper connection using their two bodies, which can even create a new human.

We are born through an act of love. No matter what happens afterwards between the two lovers, this moment of love can't be revoked. It's a profound engagement that unifies them until the end of their lives.

Besides the fact that making love can create a new life, it is also a way to express our vulnerability with someone. Indeed, sexuality can be seen as an expression of our true self.

We are naked emotionally as much as we are physically. We surrender our self in this union. We trust our partner. We unveil our main essence without any filters or safety net. It's us, fully as we are, perfect in our imperfections.

For this reason, we have the right and choice to be with someone who is from the opposite sex or the same as ours. There is no good or wrong way in sexuality, only one: the way of love. As soon as we find someone else to share our inner sanctity with in pleasure and joy, this act will be always magical.

In Family Constellations, sexuality is represented as an act of love, an act of giving and receiving.

However, sometimes, we might not be able to set up healthy boundaries.

Sexual intimacy is a privilege. When we share the details with our children, family or friends, we lose this privilege. We break this silent contract that we made with our partner. This damages respect, not only between the speaker and their partner who they share the sexual relationship with, but also in the speaker-listener relationship.

Of course, we can have fun with our friends sharing funny anecdotes but we just need to understand where the limit is and stop there. Otherwise, it creates another dynamic where boundaries are breached and people who are not part of the relationship are included unwillingly.

If we are a parent, we have to respect the sexuality of our children. We can't interfere in their process. During their childhood and adolescence, they will discover and adapt through knowledge of their own sexuality. They will become aware of their own sexual preferences and through this awareness; they will find their true self. Their sexuality might be different than ours but in any case, it needs to be accepted. By welcoming them fully as they are instead of judging them, our behavior reflects respect toward them. Adults' respectful decisions allow our children to feel more grounded.

No matter what our sexual preferences are, everyone in the family system is essentially connected or plays a role in it. Everyone has an equal value in the functioning of our sexuality. We have to understand that when we exclude someone, we actually exclude us. Plus, when someone is excluded from the family system because he's seen as 'different', this can have serious consequences on the next generations.

Even though Bert Hellinger has no specific observations regarding gay women, his observations regarding gay men indicate that they can take the place of a person who has been excluded from the system. For example, this could result if a boy assumes the place or feelings of a deceased sister when there are no female siblings in the family to do it.

So, if there was a child who died early and the child was a girl, and later on in the family there are only boys, then one of the boys has to represent a girl. By doing this, he rebalances the family system. And again, it's an act of love. It's an act of pure love for the well-being of his family lineage.

Family Constellations is a great way to see exactly where the truth lies in this particular dynamic because it is a method that avoids judgment and focuses only on healing, therefore allowing gay men and women to gain greater understanding and clarity on their true self.

Homosexuality is not an illness and in no instance does healing mean changing someone's sexuality.

Healing comes from seeing and experiencing the underlying dynamic, integrating it and coming to peace with it. Judgments have no place in constellations. It is absolutely not a means of controlling and changing other people. It is only about Love and bringing it back into the family system. Homosexuality is respected. It may be a gift of love for this person who was excluded from the family, so they can be recognized and accepted.

In our family field, we find the right distance between our parents and us. Remember, alignment with our true self is all about standing in our right place.

Through our sexuality, we express our true identity. Our sexuality belongs to us. It's our inner sanctity and a gift. Take care of it as is.

Affirmations

From the parent position:

I am the big one. You are the little one.

I am the adult. You are the child.

From the child position:

I set up boundaries with the private life of my parents.

I respect their couple relationship.

"Into-me-see"

From 0 to 6 years old, we are fully exposed to anything that happens. We feel all of the magical, dramatic events surrounding our family and us. Our body registers if love, attention, respect and kindness are present or lacking. We may not remember but our subconscious does. This is how we imprint our issues and patterns internally.

For this reason, I propose that you write up all of your memories from 0 to 6 years old.

Then, make a list of the issues you currently face as an adult. Draw a parallel between the childhood events and what you are experiencing right now in your life.

If you wish to go deeper in your healing, you can write a letter for every connection that you make.

For example, one issue in your adult life may be that you are always afraid of being abandoned. See if during your childhood, any events happened that could explain this fear of abandonment. Maybe your mom lost you at the supermarket? Or your dad was absent for one year and you never knew the reason?

By expressing our true feelings and emotions about a particular event and releasing the pain, we should experience a light mind, body and deep relief after this exercise.

Love and Bonding Are Different

During a Family Constellation, we always ask the client if her/his parents were previously married, engaged or involved in a close relationship.

Why?

Usually, within families where one or both of partners were involved in a close relationship before their married partner, the former partner is usually represented by a child of their marriage.

The children take up the cause of the former partners in the family, and often make their parents suffer for the injustice done to them. Children identify with the old partner, especially when they have been treated disrespectfully.

While doing a Family Constellation, we will be able to see if we are entangled with these kinds of situations. If so, the field will show us the dynamic and then we can work on a resolution. Remember that in Family Constellations, resolutions always have to do with Love.

For example, if the husband leaves his wife for another woman, there is a risk that the first child of this new union will carry the burden of the betrayed woman. Thus, the child could have a difficult relationship with the father or stand between the parents, defending the former mother. The child acts more as a 'lover' than a child. Plus, in his or her own relationships, the dynamic of a 3-way love affair might be possible.

Another entanglement can be seen when the parents get divorced. In order to repair the separation between their parents, the child can unconsciously take on the role of the husband or wife, or if they are old enough to get married or even pregnant, this might happen in order to fix "the failed relationship" of their parents.

Generally, a woman is more likely to stay entangled with these past dynamics than a man.

We have to pay attention to the bond with our former partners. To be able to move on, it's always nice to gain closure with this person. Making peace with him or her internally will help you to be available for a new relationship. Romanticizing the past or putting our ex-lover on a pedestal won't help another relationship materialize. So let's make room for the new one!

Plus, we can become 'entangled' with an object that represents the previous relationship, meaning unconsciously, we can stay stuck and unable to create a new bond with another lover. This object can be jewelry, a set of love letters or other mementos (theater tickets, flowers or clothing).

Don't get me wrong, we can always keep a few things from our past relationships however we have to know why we keep them. Is it out of possession, frustration or love?

Love is never tricky but the ego can make us believe it is. The ego always wants more so when you keep a bond with your past, it's only in order to feed the ego not Love.

And believe me; it took me a long time to finally understand it!

The two last examples resonate a lot with my own personal life.

My parents got divorced in January 2008, seven months after, in August 15th, 2008 I got married in Las Vegas after only two months of being in a relationship with my partner. Eight months later, I left him.

I married my partner because I wanted to 'fix' him and show him he could trust me, instead of marrying him for being the 'right man of my life'. He was very jealous, possessive and violent and I blamed myself for his feelings. A month after we met he told me I was the woman of his life and wanted to get married in Las Vegas. The idea of getting married was exciting and gained momentum in my head because I thought that Las Vegas weddings were only for fun. .

So, I said "Yes." Obviously, I was wrong. A few months of marriage is still a marriage. We can't escape that fact. I can't escape it.   As of today, my divorce is noted on my birth certificate. Yet once again, this experience made me. It led me where I wanted to go. It gave me strength. It was a chaotic revelation, but still a miracle. Sometimes, the best things in our life are born out of our shadows.

Later on, during a constellation, I finally realized that I married this man to soothe my pain from my parents' divorce. It was an act of reparation

After the divorce, I kept my engagement ring and both wedding bands. I didn't want him to keep his. My rationale at the time was that he couldn't respect the relationship with me as his wife, so how could he value these symbols? The problem was that I didn't realize that in doing this, I was keeping the bond alive with my former husband. It took me five years to finally have an epiphany regarding my decision to keep them.

One day, I woke up and I no longer felt attached to the rings. I was only attached to the protection that they offered me. So, I detached myself from this symbolic idea and moved on. I threw the rings away in the Hudson River. I love the link between emotions and water so I thought it was a very significant act to do this 'letting go' ceremony with the element of water.

Do we still feel entangled with one of our ex-lovers? Do we keep a symbol from one of our previous relationships? Is the idea of selling or throwing this object away painful? Have we been single for a long time now? Are we married to someone we don't love? Are we engaged to a man but we think about another one?

Family Constellations will help us see more clearly and understand why we keep on repeating the same behaviors.

As Mark Wolynn said, "It did not start with you but it can end with you."

Affirmations:

I will focus on loving relationships.

I forgive all past lovers; they were teachers showing me how to come home to myself.

Thank you for your love.

Rock Solid Love

We all want love. And we all deserve to have it. Whether we're weighing up a decision to end a relationship or are about to jump into a new one, or just want to get clear on what we actually want, the following exercise will help us clarify what kind of a romantic partner we are looking for.

Grab your notebook and a pen and write down answers to the following questions (replacing gender accordingly):

What qualities do you want your ideal partner to demonstrate?
How does he make me feel special?
His most important quality is...
How does he show affection?
How does he love me?
The best thing about him is...

How do you make him feel special?
Your most important quality is...
How do you show him affection?
How do you love him?
List the qualities you bring to the relationship.

Imagine you and your lover five years into the future. Use the present tense to describe your life with him.

"Abortions leave a deep trace in the soul, a very deep trace. This is often denied, with all kinds of plausible reasoning. The soul does not listen to these reasons. We say sometimes that abortion is like a kind of contraception, in Japan for instance. Still, it is experienced the same way there as it is with us here. There is no difference. It is experienced as a deep interference in the soul. The aborted children belong to the family and they are experienced that way. If this comes to light and the children are included in the family, it has a beneficial effect."
Bert Hellinger

The Womb

In Family Constellations, when we look at a person's current issues and relationships, the first important person to consider is the mother. The second important person is the mother. The third important person is the mother. The fourth person is the father.

The first three 'places' are the three generations carried at the same time of the pregnancy.

Indeed, when a woman is pregnant, she carries three generations. Her generation, her future child's generation and the generation following, which is already an aspect of her baby.

Through the role of giving birth and so the gift of life, a woman changes the world every time she delivers a child.

Even though it could be seen as a movement of a butterfly's wings, there is an impact on all of us. Who will the child become? What will their mission be? We are all connected.

It is a domino effect. We only need one to bring down others surrounding, or one to be the connecting bridge.

Women give birth to the next generations. Through this role of delivering life, women have the most powerful impact on Earth. Without women giving birth every day, humanity would disappear.

This role of women strongly impacts their relationships with men. Women also risk their life through every pregnancy and birth; therefore they can look like superheroes.

This is why it's crucial that the mother gives her husband a place in the family and trusts him to be a wonderful father.

We need two people to create a third one. And we need two people to raise a child. It's a balance. It's our child's equilibrium. Of course, a mother and a father don't have the same roles; they interlock their positions to form the parental unit.

It is important to value both people during the raising: and likewise during the pregnancy period. No matter what happens - abortion, miscarriage, stillborn or full-term birth – they are together. It was a common decision. Two adults felt the strong desire to procreate, no matter how that life ultimately unfolded.

By becoming parents, we face our own death; this is why we create another generation because we know life is uncertain, so our children will survive us. Normally this is the order. Unfortunately, sometimes life has another plan and our child dies before us. I can't imagine the pain but the gift of life is precious and we must honor it. As we respect our life, we respect the end of it. Once born, we already know that one day, we will die. By accepting this fact, we grant ourselves permission to fully live our life.

In the case of an abortion, both parents must give a place to this child in their heart. Otherwise, their relationship is likely to break up quickly. It has to be a common decision and one that is deeply respected afterwards.

One very important observation is that a child who follows an abortion might feel anxious. This is due to the fact that the child feels guilty about living. "Why me?" "Why am I alive and not my sibling?"

Parents should pay attention to this anxiety as it could lead to an addiction or some other risk-taking behavior, with the hidden goal of assuaging the guilt. Generally, this dynamic happens when a child follows an abortion; however, sometimes it takes place with a child who precedes an abortion. In this case, the older sibling has the subconscious feeling that he or she should have saved the younger sibling.

Miscarriage – a horrible world as my teacher Suzi Tucker points out, could be rewritten as "mis-carry." The mother of course unconsciously feels that she did something wrong, that she didn't carry the baby appropriately.

Again, we blame the mother. We judge her for her inability to carry this baby to full term. Often, the father can blame the mother too. A separation can result from this dangerous, unfair and blind behavior.

It is a similar issue when we think about stillborn children; there can be plenty of reproaches between the parents.

Instead of jointly bearing this fate, they assign the fault to each other. The pain of a repressed mourning separates the parents but also the other children. A great parenthood finds its roots in having children while simultaneously accepting the loss of a child and mutually bearing this destiny. This allows the heart to have room for everyone.

When mourning has its place, Love can express itself.

All of the members of a family have the same right to belong to it and so the unborn child does too. When we recognize the death, we accept our own destiny and its limits. By giving a place to our unborn child, we allow him or her to be at peace and therefore, we make peace with our loss. Agree to the child's fate. Let Love take care of everyone -- Mother, Father, living children and those who did not make it.

It's also not recommended to stay focused on a child's death. By idealizing the deceased child, we other children will feel excluded, and the idealized one will feel burdened.

The following stories illustrate the importance of taking care of ourselves when we are pregnant, so there are no repercussions on our child's life.

While I don't have enough distance and awareness to talk about twins in the context of Family Constellations yet in more detail, I wanted to share this story.

One of my friends lost her twin when their mother was pregnant with them. One consequence of this loss seems to be that now my friend always needs another person with her. She needs to recreate a 'twinship', whether with a friend or a lover. She simply needs to feel accompanied by another person.

Can we see how powerful it is to share the same space? How much impact it can have on our life? Even though my friend never met her twin physically, she lived a spiritual and intimate connection with her. A deep bond was made during this quick period of gestation.

When my mother was seven months pregnant, she fell under a train. She had the reflex to protect her belly so to protect me. She was not hurt. When I was three months old, my mom went to pick up my father at the train station. When the train was arriving, I cried out fearfully. For sure as a fetus I felt the fear of my mother, and experienced my own trauma reaction inside the womb. The subconscious remembers!

When one of my friends was pregnant, she established this lovely routine to dance every night to the same song. She told me that for her it was "their" moment and that when her daughter felt anxious or angry, she was going to play this music. And it turned out that once her daughter was born, any time she felt grumpy, the music had this magical power to calm her down instantly.

What about you? Do you have any lovely stories to share with your children?

Affirmations

Between the parents:

We bear this pain together.

We accept your destiny and we will keep following ours.

You belong to our family.

The Light that Comes with Mourning

For an abortion, miscarriage or stillbirth, the first meaningful thing to do is a little ceremony to recognize the child and also acknowledge our own pain.

You can write a letter and even give your baby a name or you can write the name on a balloon along with your wish for his or her life. Wherever your baby is, they will feel the love. When Love is here, the pain will go away.

For the death of a child, you can place a picture of him or her in your kitchen or your family room, so you can let him or her be at peace even as you mourn.

Recognizing our pain and our loss is a better, easier way to keep moving forward on the path of our destiny.

The Interrupted Movement

When the child's movement to the mother is interrupted at an early age – that is when the mother is felt to be missing in the child's formative years – the child becomes afraid and angry. The early interrupted movement is a period from 0 to six years old where the child has been abandoned by his mother and/or father, which could be due to a hospitalization, abandonment, adoption, or the death of one of the parents. This comes through any kind of separation, because the very young child cannot make a distinction between one kind of absence and another.

Generally, this 'interrupted movement' is related to the mother; however we also see cases of an interrupted movement with the father.

Interrupted mother-child bonding is dramatic and can have long-lasting effects. The child might keep their anger or rage against the mother for "leaving" until the movement has been healed. Indeed, the child's anger and rejection of the mother is fear-driven and deeply hidden in the subconscious. The child learns that if he reaches out, nobody reaches back, so eventually the child stops reaching out and even pushes others away in order to preempt their abandonment of him. This anger is a protection against being hurt again. To be able to break the curse or pattern, the child will need to live through this interrupted movement again and finally close it so that a feeling of completion can take over.

If we are aware of the situation and the child is still young, we could do the following: sit him or her on our lap and embrace the child tightly until we feel no more resistance.

Repeat this powerful hug of love in expectation of a complete resolution in his or her behavior. Also, follow this new movement by paying attention to being consistent in our behavior toward the child, like being on time to pick the child up, being clear and regular about normal daily transitions – going to bed, school and play dates. As we embraced the child tightly, embrace this new behavioral shift tightly and consistently.

If we know we were separated from our mother at an early age, we can set up a Family Constellation where the facilitator will ask the person representing our mother to embrace our neck and touch it in small circles, gently and lovingly. This recreates the movement of love that was disrupted between us and our mother. We can also hold the right hand of our mother's representative in the field and walk in circles together. This will lead to the resolution.

These two pieces of advice relate to the healing of the inner child/child. If our mother tried to have an abortion or didn't want us when she was pregnant, we need to work on reconnecting with our fetus because this area of the body is where the emotions of this trauma are stored. It takes more time because we have to find our inner fetus in our body. It begins with the realization that things that occur when we are very young may be forgotten by the mind, but not by the body.

Remember, it's our job to keep sparking and growing our inner light regardless of our pain, abuse, dramas or abandonment. It is one of our fundamental rights to be proud of our life. Let's celebrate it every day! I understand this is always easier said than done, yet, this is the only way to live an abundant, serene life.

The more willing we are to accept self-love and self-respect from our 'inner mother', the easier it will be for us to come to a resolution.

If we don't accept our mother and nurture this link with our inner one, we may look for another form of love through drugs, sex, alcohol or another addiction. When we reject our parents, we reject ourselves because we are made from our parents.

We have the ability to heal all our scars through various ways that reveal our life's importance and our light to us.

We are important. We are loved. We are light.

Affirmations

I am loved.

I recreate the circle of love between my mother and me.

When I am connected with my inner mother, I am at peace.

Hold Me Tight

Ask your mother to embrace your neck and make gentle circles with her fingers on this area. If your mother is not ready or you prefer, you can ask another person whom you trust and feel safe with, or even do this yourself, making the circles as your inner mother until you feel peace inside you. If touching your neck feels uncomfortable, ask for a tight, long hug.

It is important to mother our inner child as an adult. We are the guide. The child needs us to heal and release any negative feelings that were experienced during childhood.

When our inner child is at peace, the adult we are will be as well. When the adult reaches out to provide shelter, the inner child will be at peace. This is another circle of love.

If your child is agitated, violent or quick-tempered, I advise you to hug him or her tight when the child is experiencing one of those 'out-of-control' moments. At first, he or she will probably refuse your embrace but don't let go. You will see your child relax and feel safe after time. Keep embracing your child until the uncontrollable urge passes.

Love is the antidote for everything. The more we lose patience in front of our child, they more they will become agitated.

We don't fight violence with more violence. We calm down violence with Love.

"Was it the act of giving birth that made you a mother? Did you lose that label when you relinquished your child? If people were measured by their deeds, on the one hand, I had a woman who had chosen to give me up; on the other, I had a woman who'd sat up with me at night when I was sick as a child, who'd cried with me over boyfriends, who'd clapped fiercely at my law school graduation. Which acts made you more of a mother? Both. I realized. Being a parent wasn't just about bearing a child. It was about bearing witness to its life."

Jodi Picoult

Adoption: Agreeing to What Is

Adoption has many complex dynamics and movements behind the scenes that need to be known, recognized and fully accepted, in order to provide stability for the adopted child once it is in a new family system.

As Bert Hellinger said: "People who were adopted are a challenge. They have blunted emotions. It is much easier for them to act than to feel. A tree whose roots were cut has difficulty putting up new roots. The stress of getting disconnected with parents is one of the most severe stresses in life no matter how good the adoptive parents are."

For this reason and despite the beautiful act of love of adopting a child, adoptive parents have to be aware of the principle of order, meaning biological parents are first. Without them, there would be no child. There needs to be a silent agreement between them.

"Even though the biological parents lose their rights, they don't lose their place." The adoptive parents must respect the biological parents. Only in this esteem, can they respect the child. In this process and in a conscientious way the adoptive parents should say silently to the biological parents: 'Thanks to you I can become a parent'," notes Suzi Tucker.

By doing this silent ceremony, the adoptive parents recognize the role of the biological parents, thus the child will have enough room to love all of his parents in his heart. He or she will be fully aware of the situation and will release their anger.

An adopted child is always angry on some level with the biological parents for abandoning them. Deep within, the child is very upset with them and this resentment often transfers to the adoptive parents. This transfer might create stressful, challenging situations in the adoptive family.

We have to understand that an adoption, energetically speaking, is like an abortion. We give the child up and the child has to accept that he or she also needs to give their biological parents up in order to live a more beautiful, serene life. The adopted child needs to consent to what the parents decided. Only through this awareness and consent can an adopted child grow up serenely.

Despite this anger, the child has to accept that he or she can love its new parents without feeling guilty. More often, an adopted child will feel it's betraying its biological parents and therefore is unable to appreciate and love his or her new home.

It is often more difficult when a couple adopts a child from another country with a different culture to their own, as this removes the child from its natural family, community and nation. Before adopting a child, we must check that there aren't other family members in its homeland – grandparents, aunt or uncle – who could take care of this child. Only when there is no family member willing and able to take care of the child, can we seek other parents or carers elsewhere. Generally, it is always better for the child to be raised in his or her's native culture.

The biological parents must also bear their responsibility and choice entirely to avoid confusion and blame. If the parents sit on the fence, it will be destructive for the child: "I don't have time for you now but I will be back." The child will be confused and unable to settle with this ambivalence; he/ she won't know where to belong or have peace. This is why there is no possible return for the biological parents after adoption has been decided. Adoption is the adults' decision. Their child has no responsibility in this act and doesn't have to bear this choice or atone for them.

In the case of a surrogate for sterile or homosexual couples, the donor has to be recognized in the family system. Without this recognition, the child will perhaps bear a heavy weight. Hellinger doesn't have any more specific observations or insights on this dynamic yet. Nonetheless in this century, we will soon discover what's going on inside this 'new' family type.

Divorces and separations can often follow an adoption. It is not the regular system so the agreement between the parents turns out differently. For example, the adoption is a reminder that the woman is sterile, the man is "unable" or that the parents waited too long. Sometimes adoption can push us back into our shadows and the different burdens that we had during childhood, so then the couple becomes strangers to each other.

It's critical to share the truth with our child. We have to tell her or him that he/she was adopted. We can't take away his or her right to know. How could we expect him or her to find their place? The child will always know in one corner of its mind that something is askew.

If we are an adopted child, we may have to accept that our biological parents will refuse to see us again. We can't take this personally. Their refusal often stems from the fact that they do not have the courage to see their own guilt again in our eyes.

All of these insights on adoption aside, I concur with Suzi Tucker who says that adoption is the best *way* the biological parents could find to 'parent' and allow the child to live. So, it's essential that the biological and adoptive parents express silent gratitude for each other in a reciprocal act. Secondly, if children are encouraged and allowed to love the biological parents openly, they are less likely to find covert, destructive ways: "I'll be a junkie like my junkie mother!", or, "I am a no-good idiot like my father so why try!"

Acceptance, as always, is the fastest way to move on and wholeheartedly live our life.

Affirmations

For the adoptive parents:

Thanks to you I can become a parent.

I respect you as the biological father.

I respect you as the biological mother.

For the adopted child:

I have enough room in my heart to love all my parents.

By accepting and respecting your decision, I agree to move on.

I let you go with love.

Homeland

If you are from a different culture and country than your adopted parents, it might be good for you to plan a trip to your homeland. By discovering your roots and putting your feet on your natural home ground, you might find your "spiritual" place in this world. It is important to know where we came from to move forward on our path. You could also propose that your adopted parents participate in this trip.

During your stay, bring a journal to write your thoughts and emotions. You could also collect a few things, such as shells, plants, flowers, sand, or soil from your homeland to take back with you. It could be anything or memento, as long as it feels important to you.

By reconnecting with your roots, you will feel more steady and grounded in your adopted country.

We Are All Different Together

Often, we think we can't deal with challenges or tough situations. The truth is: we can deal with anything. We have enough strength to adapt to every incident that comes to us. Naturally, we can sometimes feel devastated, lost, blocked or disappointed but at some point, if we keep moving, we realize that will make it. If we refuse to move, instead staying with old images and ideals, the challenges may defeat us, not because they are so big but because we have stayed small and stuck.

Every missing link will be found and all together, they create a complete life. Life can be seen as a treasure hunt – at the end, it's what we found during the search that is the real treasure.

So focus on the search or journey, not the prize. The prize only represents all of the obstacles we jumped over and embraced. We must value our endless commitment and movement for our life above all. Enjoy the ride and focus on the journey over the destination, as the destination often morphs into something different or opposite than we first envisioned, generally for the better.

Throughout our life, we will change, meet new people and say goodbye to others; we will love, hate, believe, lose faith, celebrate a birth and mourn a dearly departed one. This is the cycle of life with its ups and downs, narrow and spacious ways, expectations and disappointments, joys and pains.

Life is not easy and can even be very uncomfortable at times but everything will make sense at the end of the day.

Are we all equals when it comes to achieving something? Yes. I believe everyone has a specific, unique mission. This mission or purpose belongs to us and even though we may want to achieve the same thing, each person will do it differently.

Our difference is precious. Through our differences, we learn from each other. Difference creates unity – unity between us, animals, Mother Nature and humankind. It's when we don't accept our difference that a gap forms with other people.

We are all part of the same history. We are together in that. Our behavior has a rebound effect on others. And this rebound behavior effect happens in family systems. One behavior, good or bad, will always have a repercussion on the current generation, as well as the next ones that follow. For as long as someone ignores or does not recognize this behavior or act, it will keep on going. This behavior will actually happen in more situations to help us resolve and release the underlying issue and if we are not able to see or acknowledge it, we resist and therefore continue creating more dramas and painful situations.

We might become disabled in front of love, joy, abundance and so on, which means we are not able to face and embrace it. Anger, sadness, revenge, meanness, resentment and more will begin to be a part of our normal state, which is where disabilities come from. Physical and intellectual differences can spur us on or sink us in the quicksand of negative feelings.

By not seeing love as it is and what life can offer, we become disabled and disconnected from the world. We see ourselves as victims, causing internal chaos. At first, the rift may be small but by feeding our rage, we enlarge the crack and create more and more disastrous situations.

The real 'obstacles' are not the ones we see, they are the ones that hide inside and afflict us little by little. These challenges hide in able and disabled bodies alike.

We are the only ones who can enable our goals and dreams. No one else has the power to guide our life. We represent our own choices and if we think we can't do it, for sure, we won't. But, if we know we can do it, no matter what crosses our road, we will overcome any challenges and reach our goal.

We give ourselves the love that people show us. We give ourselves our own limits and parameters. We make the best of the opportunities that come to us. We are a magnet; we attract what we think we are. When we enable our mind to think bigger, a lot of great things will happen.

There are a hundred ways to accomplish something. Do we want to enable or disable all the options by keeping a rigid view? The choice is ours.

Affirmations

This is our child. We will take care of him/her together and will respond to his/her needs as his/her parents.

You belong to your family.

Thank you for bringing love back into our family.

You are. I am.

Put your book on the table and take a few minutes to look around you. Which color is most dominant where you are right now? Do you smell anything in particular? A coffee, apple pie, or a delicate perfume?

What about your body? Do you feel fully present in this moment? Do you feel connected with yourself? Your thoughts? Your world?

What can you do right now to empower your day?

Make this pause and sensory check-in an essential part of your daily routine. It will allow you to focus on the essential and tune into yourself, allowing you to perhaps make another decision or take a few steps back from an unhealthy situation.

By making room for yourself, you claim your affiliation to this world; you claim your difference, uniqueness and who you are.

Root of all Evil

The majority of our physical boo-boos, scratches, pains, diseases, grazes, injuries and hurts are often linked with suppressing one of our negative emotions. All chronic physical problems have systemic, internal roots. Our role: uproot them!

Are we angry? Sad? Depressed? Disappointed? If so, we could go beyond our present circumstances to consider what happened in the past and ask ourselves: "Why is my inner child X (write your emotion – angry / sad / hurt / jealous)?" The root of this feeling can be blocked in our inner child and our body is physically manifesting it and trying to get rid of it. This could just be the flu, an ache or even more serious illnesses.

For example, Hellinger discovered in Family Constellations that sometimes breast cancer is an atonement for the injustice done to a man. Food addictions (binge eating, Anorexia, and Bulimia) are often related with abuse and sexual harassment. Degenerative diseases (Alzheimer's, Parkinson's, Dementia) are connected to the desire to go back into childhood to escape the difficulties of present daily life. In removing themselves from the present, people with these conditions can be seen to heal their past and therefore their inner child in a way, who was traumatized by a profound event, such as war, abuse, or suicide affecting either themselves or their family system.

Headaches are usually caused by love that is unable to flow. Perhaps as a child, our access or movement towards the mother was interrupted before we reached our goal or had our needs met. This early interrupted movement was described in an earlier chapter, and refers to separation from our mother/father through abandonment, hospitalization, divorce or death during our early development phase (0 to 6 years old). This is one possible cause of our headaches linked to underlying anger or aggressiveness towards the mother.

Shoulders can hold feelings of anger and conflict with others in the body. If we are experiencing pain in our shoulders, let's ask ourselves, "Who do I want to slap?" Generally, if the suffering is located in our right side, the anger or conflict in the shoulder is against a man; on the left side, the anger is against a woman.

If we ever think about committing suicide, we can ask:, "Who do I want to save?" We are probably entangled with someone who passed away before our birth and in loyalty to our family system; we want to follow that person.

Backaches tend to represent the pain of not feeling supported by our family. "Who do I have to bow to?" This is an important consideration, even though we think this person might not deserve bowing to. Scoliosis is often caused by a divorce or by being raised by parents from different cultures and because we can't make a choice. Our spine tries to adjust itself between two different cultures or people. Rather than integrate, we try to balance separate entities.

Our eyes hold the soul of our parents. The left eye is our mother's soul and the right eye is our father's soul. When we have difficulty seeing, let's ask ourselves, "What is it in my mother or father that I don't want to face?"

If we make a fist with our hands, this generally means we are repressing anger. Let's ask ourselves, "Why am I feeling angry while I am talking with him/her?"

When our body shivers and we are not freezing temperature wise, this means our body is expelling fears. The shaking releases repressed fears.

A heavy calf can describe an unspoken sadness.

Being anxious is the same feeling as being excited -- with a dash of fear. "What am I afraid of?"

When we get sick, this is often because we aren't feeling confident enough about a meeting a person or a situation and so to avoid it, we get sick!

To summarize, let's ask ourselves, "Where do I feel pain?"

Try to focus on this pain in our mind and breathe very deeply until we feel it easing off. If not, I recommend buying Louise Hay's book, *You Can Heal Your Life.* This book provides great insight into our body and our different pains.

Our body is our best doctor. Pay attention to its signs. By becoming our body's friend, we will avoid a lot of undesirable, useless suffering.

Affirmations

I love all my emotions. They all have a purpose.

I listen to my body.

I am worthy of experiencing my feelings.

Scan Your Body

It's time to listen to your body. Scan your body from head to toe. Where do you feel tension? Describe the feeling linked to this tension. Give the feeling a color or a texture. Be as descriptive as possible. The feeling you're describing is the old insecurity and fear that lives underneath your need to control. That feeling was never healed so you think you need to control it. Take 60 seconds to just breathe into the feeling wherever it lives in your body, then let it go.

You can even silently talk to your body using these phrases: "I calm my body", "I liberate my body", "I am free from anger, fear and anxiety", "I am aware of my whole body".

Feeding the Love

"Finish your plate, then you can watch TV, "If you don't eat your spinach, you won't become strong," "Don't eat cookies, you will become fat."

Having a peaceful relationship with food can be hard to put in practice as an adult, especially if food was experienced as a manipulation, demand or even punishment in our childhood. .

Until the age of 12, I had good memories sharing my meals with my family, grandparents and friends. However, when my brother left for boarding school, I started feeling very uncomfortable sitting down for lunch or dinner with my parents. I would eat faster to avoid my one-on-one time with my parents. I had this feeling that I was not in my place. My brother missed me a lot; he was the funny one in the family, always making jokes. He was my sunshine, my private comic. He was my brother and I felt in balance in relation to my parents besides him at the dining table.

As soon as this familiar routine stopped, I started another one: bingeing. After I had finished my meal, I would run to my bedroom and eat cookies compulsively. I was not hungry for food. I was only hungry for Love. I was trying to feed myself to feel love inside of me and feel complete.

Without my brother, I did not feel like a sister anymore. I felt incomplete. In my mind, I remember it as the beginning of the end of our family. Six years later, my parents got divorced.

I was aware of my behavior with food; I was aware of my pain however I didn't want to face it. Years and years past before I could finally make peace with my body and it's still a fragile relationship. I feel like Bambi on the skating rink. I make great efforts but I am wary of falling.

The difference now is I am able to immediately recognize the precursory signs. Moody, sad, lonely, depressed; these feelings can be a definite trigger to go hunting for cookies! Now however, I am able to calm myself down and focus another activity to provide comfort, such as meditating, running, reading, bathing. This works pretty well for me.

I still need to make peace with food and the idea of being the perfect women according to the rules of others or society at large. Again, this is just a matter of loving myself as I am! Nothing else! I cook to create a relationship with food, I think it's important to feel comfortable in a kitchen and take pleasure in cooking.

When I started working on this issue, I realized that when you enjoy doing something it's hard to feel guilty.

Bingeing for me was a way to look for love. Overeating was a way to fill myself with love, to feel full. The aftermath was the worst part of this behavior of course, where I only felt connected to my old buddies 'guilt', 'shame' and 'you look so fat!' instead of love...not really the result I wanted!

Through different therapies, I have learned that our relationship with our bodies and food is entangled with the relationship we have to our mother. There is a strong correlation between our weight and this relationship. Again, 'poor mom' we might think, for contributing to another pattern like an eating disorder! Let's remember once again that our mother did the best she could.

So first, we need to heal the relationship with our mother, and then we can start doing the work on ourself.

Healing the relationship with our mom will immediately impact how we visualize ourself.

Having an eating disorder is painful and hard to handle but I am convinced that with a lot of love and compassion for our pattern, we can get better day after day.

It's still challenging for me but I try to indulge those moments and send more love to myself.

Patience is part of the process. Eating with pleasure marks the beginning of a new and serene relationship with our body.

Please refer to the appendix for more resources on where to find help for an eating disorder.

Affirmations

My food is a blessing.

I celebrate the gift of life.

As I take care of my body, I take care of myself.

Mindfulness

I used to be a pretty fast-paced lady: I talked fast, worked fast, ate fast and moved fast. I always did things fast because I didn't like the idea of 'wasting my time'. Finally, I had an 'aha moment' and realized that it was time to enjoy and savor my life! I became more mindful and present in my « now ». I started eating more slowly and mindfully. Believe me, it's an awesome experience!

Now, every time when I eat, I allow my taste buds to fully experience the flavors. I pay attention to nothing other than what is going on in my mouth in that moment.

It's life changing!

So, for this reason, I'd suggest you have a mindfulness date with your next meal. Cook something that you love and take time to experience every mouthful. Feel your body fill up little by little. Rediscover the taste of the food. Pick an adjective to describe the flavor of your food, be it an apple or vodka pasta sauce...

Be in the present moment!

Birds in One Cage

It is natural to experience various emotions in certain situations. Our emotions are necessary to help us feel and express ourselves as human beings. Emotions only become a problem if they stay frozen in a traumatic event...and because we didn't have the chance to express ourselves at that time, it becomes a burden.

From a Family Constellations perspective, if we suffer with an emotional issue, we may be entangled with one or more family members, so it could be more than just a personal, internal problem.

In my family, we didn't talk often about our emotions and feelings. We were very reserved regarding our own personal struggles and troubles. When we wanted to share something, we wrote letters and to show our love, we offered gifts. It was our family thing or way of communicating.

My brother and I express our feelings by sending songs. I wish I could talk with him more, but as long as we still have a connection, I will accept this concept as a compromise.

Words can be fierce, so sometimes, it's better to keep our words within and take our time to align our words with more care, rather than just being reactive. Then we can have more constructive conversations.

I was afraid of my emotions and therefore, the power of my

words. I didn't want to hurt my mother or good friends so I kept my feelings and words inside me, repressed. Unfortunately, this behavior led to my depression, which I experienced for almost a decade. It's important to realize that with depression, we are not conscious when we start our descent into it. Depression is shrouded in total denial. We know we are suffering but because we don't see any blood or cuts, we think it will pass like a grumpy mood. Days can easily turn into months and even years, if the depression is not recognized and treated.

It's always harder when we can't see things but only feel them. I felt lost, afraid and frozen. I had no more appetite. I felt empty. I had no desire, no envy. In fact, the only one desire I had was to protect my family. I felt good at it and maybe it was convenient for them as well. For me, this silent agreement was an act of love and also a diversion or denial that if I didn't say I was depressed out loud, that meant it did not exist.

I pretended I was fine but on the inside, my feelings of emptiness turned into sorrow. Sorrow at not knowing what I wanted to do, sorrow at being dependent on others, sorrow at hiding my emotions. This sorrow lay inside a huge scream that needed to come out but that I was repressing more and more. I was burning up because I couldn't express my suffering. I will never forget the sensation of having this heaviness sensation within my stomach. It was like carrying a huge ball of depression, suffering and unhappiness every day. I can't clearly remember when I dropped this 'ball' but I know for sure that it is not a part of me anymore.

This ball of depression was my way to feel alive. When we feel pain, we know we are alive and even though I was miserable, I still felt alive.

I don't know exactly how I got through that period. I know I had awesome friends and family, I guess I took strength from them. I was more concerned about their suffering than mine and I am sure it saved me.

I focused on them, not myself. They were my breath, my oxygen, my smile, my love and while I had them, I could feel useful. And then I decided to move to America with my husband at the time. I was no longer in love with him but I know I needed him. I needed him to feel useful. He was more destroyed than I was so as long as I was dedicated to taking care of his troubles; I was able to comfortably distract myself from mine.

One day, the truth hit me. I couldn't help him anymore, otherwise I felt like I was killing myself, little by little. So after another dispute, he left our place and during those few hours alone, I knew that my cage had been left opened and it was my chance to leave him. I packed my things and left with a heavy heart. I didn't know where to go but I knew that I was not alone in this new move. I was like a little bird trying to fly on its own.

It was not easy. And truthfully, I went back to him a few times. Even now, I don't clearly know why. I guess I needed his pain to locate myself. As soon as I could catch him in my web, it was exhilarating. Actually, it felt pretty pathetic but I didn't care. All I wanted was for him to look at me so I could see his love for me. I loved this silent attachment between us. It was intense, dramatic, full of tears, screaming and very sexual. I loved all of that. I was a dramatic heroine and I was addicted to this role. I didn't want to leave the stage, to stop my movie, but fortunately, I grew tired of it. I became aware that I was digging my hole deeper and deeper, and that I was the only one capable of stopping the process.

To stop the process, I had to make peace with men and my past. I didn't want to be that woman who hates men, but I was on this road and I didn't know how to make a U-turn. I hated them. I hated him. It was so unfair that at 13 years old a man had taken away my dreams, hope, youth and my innocence. In my mind, that man equaled all men.

Sometimes, I have those moments when I ask myself, "Where would I be today if nothing had happened? What kind of woman would I have been? Would I be married already? And with children?" But then I remember that the past is the past. You can't change your destiny or your past, so you just need do the best you can and enjoy the ride. My story from the past does not define who I am today; I am the one who defines myself.

I chose to survive and create something beautiful from my experiences. I triumphed by moving and making small steps. I kept going in movement through my pain, my scars, my oppression, my depression and my broken heart. It was hard but in the end it was worth it. In those years, I kept believing in something that I couldn't see or touch – a conviction that I needed to save myself to serve the world.

I wanted to be someone and I am doing it right now. I don't remember when my depression went away exactly, but one morning I woke up and felt different. I felt more grounded and connected. There was no magic wand but I suddenly recognized the reward for staying with the movement, where I gradually gathered strength, gratitude and belief in myself. Realistically I know that there will be times when I will feel a bit depressed and moody but I will be fine because the worst is behind me. My blind spots are part of the past. I know that I am strong now and the keeper of my own boundaries.

We must protect and honor our own essence. We are beautiful. We are enough. We are smart. What happened to us in the past or potentially in the future will never be our true identity. They are only experiences and we have the power to change them in a positive way. How we paint the events that occur is most important. We can paint our life's experiences in black, or we can paint them in other shades - pink, yellow, green or blue. Yes, sometimes 'black' will be here but let's see it as a reminder that our life is very colorful. Contradictions are beautiful. They are here to show us our blessings. Without comparison, how could we be aware of all the options and the more brightly colored events, people and times in our life?

During my rehabilitation, I read widely about depression and emotional issues. I resonated with David Servan-Schreiber's amazing book, "The Instinct to Heal". Servan-Schreiber was the first one to write about depression and he proposed that depression was not a fatality – if we wanted to heal from it, we had the capacity to do so. The main idea was that depression can be beaten by taking actions; by being in movement.

When we are in movement, we don't think, we just act. We can be paralyzed by our thoughts but never by our actions. And this truth helped me a lot in my recovery.

Throughout my learning process, I realized that depression is always a feeling of emptiness, not sorrow. Sometimes depression is caused by internal conflict or unexpressed emotions, however depression can also result from family dynamics that we are caught up in. This is especially valid if one of the parents has been shut out through illness, absence or death. Identifying the dynamic and situation that needs treatment can help to resolve the underlying stressors of depression and other mental illnesses.

The best way is to accept our parents as they are. There is always healing when we give a place to the excluded or rejected parent back in our heart. Again, we have to fully accept the parent as he or she is and also understand that perhaps the depression was the best way we could find to stay connected to them.

We won't lose our identity by accepting our mom or dad because depression is not our identity. It is only a statement of where we are right now, when we feel powerless, lost or disconnected with our life.

I love Family Constellations because it allows us to get to the root of an issue and resolve it there, so that managing our emotions linked to that issue is no longer necessary and we can return to good health. We are able to make the essential transformation "from blind love to enlightened love" that Bert Hellinger identified.

Affirmations

I commit to supporting and strengthening myself and others today.

I am supported as I ask for help.

I will be in touch with my feelings

Blossom by Knowing Your Roots

Do you know where your grandparents grew up? Do you know where your mom and dad went to high school? Do you know where your parents met? Do you know if there was an illness in your family, or a terrible event that happened? Do you know the story of your birth? If not, it's time to ask your family questions! You will enjoy writing the story of your family. You could buy a beautiful notebook to present to your children, grandchildren, and other family members, where everyone can write something about their own generation. It will become your family book to be passed down.

Redirecting the Energy

"An addiction is a condition that results when a person ingests a substance (alcohol, cocaine, nicotine) or engages in an activity (gambling) that can be pleasurable but the continued use of which becomes compulsive and interferes with ordinary life responsibilities, such as work or relationships, or one's health. Users may not be aware that their behavior is out of control and causing problems for themselves and others." Psychology Today

Often, we think of addiction only in relation to drugs, alcohol and sex. Addiction is much broader than that. We can be addicted to gambling, exercise, TV, eating green vegetables or cleanliness ...the list goes on! Anything can become an addiction when we take a behavior beyond normal limits to the extreme.

For example, exercising a few hours a week is healthy. Spending four or five hours a day doing cardio, boxing or yoga is not healthy if we are not a professional athlete. This is too much for our body, it needs to rest. If we are in this pattern, we must ask ourselves what we are looking for through this constant search for perfection.

Treating ourselves to the occasional cookie or cheese plate is healthy. If we only eat greens or follow an extremely restrictive diet however, once again, there is a disorder in feeding our body.

Watching our favorite TV show every Thursday is one thing, yet it's another if we put off other activities consistently to just watch TV. What are we afraid of? Contact with people or real life?

It's one thing to believe in astrology and angels. It's another thing to wait for signs and messages from them before we get out of bed, cross the road or call this guy! Why can't we make the decision on our own?

Addiction is defined by doing or taking something too much. Once it gets to this stage, there is no more pleasure in the crutch of choice only dependence. " I can't live without it". "I can't feel good in my own skin without it". "I will lose my job without it". "I can't be happy without it".

We may think a certain behavior or addiction is healthy, but personally I don't make a distinction between someone who takes cocaine to someone who only eats strawberries or watches TV all the time! An issue or something unresolved is hiding behind these behaviors. We might feel bad about ourselves or uncomfortable with a particular someone or situation in our life, so our addiction takes charge of it.

How do we know when a behavior is an addiction? When we can't get through our day without doing this specific routine or behavior; when our emotional system needs the habit/s to feel safe.

An addiction is a metaphor for one or several of our fears. Addictions appear when we don't have enough strength to deal with our life, when we are afraid to face it. Addiction is like a cuddly toy except at a certain point; we begin to play dangerously with our life.

Life can be tough, disappointing, sad, unfair, and violent. Life can also be loving, joyful, happy, fair, and fun. It's a question of perception.

I was addicted to anxiolytics for a couple years. I thought they were helping me face my world and fears. However, I discovered that when their effects wore off, my fears came back. The escape only lasted a few hours. So, I took another pill, then another and another. At the end of the day, my world looked like a surreal 'Teletubbies' world. I messed up my studies, first loves, body, self-love, self-confidence and self-esteem. I was addicted to feeling good quickly but could not find an enduring solution. I was afraid to cry or ask for help. I was scared to confess to my family that I was suffering so much. So, I chose to be an addict and pretend that everything was fine.

The truth is, life is not rainbows and butterflies every day. Life is tough but rest assured, we can face the challenges and obstacles that appear in our way. We will handle them because we are enough, complete and perfect as we are.

During Family Constellation workshops, when I have a client who comes for addictions, I am always asking myself "What's happened to her little girl or his little boy that they think they are not worth it?"

Being an addict is like holding a huge, troublesome flag every day, telling the world that we are suffering and don't know what to do.

It took me several years to stop taking anxiolytics, so I know how hard it can be. To finally say STOP takes great courage. I can't guarantee it will be easy but by asking for help, we will take the first step toward our recovery. One new movement can change our life. Take a different step and we will see how our life responds with a new, wondrous path.

Lastly, for those who have a family member struggling with an addiction, the best advice I received from my teacher Suzi Tucker is to: "Love her. Love her fate." "Love him. Love his fate."

We are here to be an example, not a judge. We are not here to fix neither save the world.

We have to respect the fate of our family, friends and others. They have a soul and purpose. Each one of us has a level of consciousness that seeks to be expanded and their choice of expansion has to be respected, honored and appreciated.

By seeing them as victims, we dishonor their journey. By seeing their suffering like they lack something, we exclude them. Let's bow with a deep respect towards their experience, to their contribution and let them go on to their destiny. This respects them instead of crying helplessly for them.

And this behavior will make all the difference.

Affirmations

I am not here to save the world neither to be saved.

I love you. I love your fate.

I am here to accept my family.

Love Them. Love Their Fate.

How can I help my sister? How can I help my father? You can't imagine how many times I have heard this question from my clients who were feeling useless and helpless about a close family member facing addiction.

My first question is: Does he/she want to be helped?

Often, the answer is "No". And with a "no" you can't do anything for him or her. So in that particular case, the advice that I give is "Love him. Love his fate. Love her. Love her fate."

By accepting his/her destiny, you won't be in a position of judgment, so then the person may feel safer to open her/his heart and finally ask for help.

The Call of Ghosts

Suicide is defined as "The act or an instance of intentionally killing oneself," (The Free Dictionary by Farlex)

My first question regarding this classic, textbook definition: Is it fully intentional?

I have some doubt on the inclusion of 'intentional' in this definition, since studying Family Constellations and Transgenerational therapy.

In Family Constellations, when someone wants to commit suicide, this often means that he or she is entangled with someone in the family who may have been murdered, committed suicide or even disappeared without any further acknowledgment by the family. In other words, when someone is missing in the family system, someone has to atone for it. This can be discovered through signs – an awkward behavior, tendency to flirt with death through repetitive accidents such as car accident, multiple fractures or a deep depression. The first questions we should consider are: "Who does he /she imitate?" "Who does he/she want to follow?"

We can find precursors for suicide in behaviors that seem "normal" or "safe" at first, but actually have deeper emotional charges.

For example, if a child doesn't want to go to school anymore, ask him or her why? In his or her subconscious, there could be some reason that stops him or her from going. "Why should I go to school if I am going to die soon?"

or "What is the point of learning new skills?" Here, the child sees the simple routine of going to school as useless. The child has no more desire to learn because he/ she has little energy to live. As we can see, this seemingly innocent behavior, unless investigated, could hide a bigger situation where the child is actually suffering a lot and trying to find a meaning for his or her life.

The reasons for suicide are often deeply unconscious and the very definition of suicide itself is also one that lives outside the sphere of most peoples' awareness. That is, one doesn't have to jump from a bridge or swallow poison to be engaged in the process of stopping life.

In Western society, piercings and tattoos are other behaviors to pay attention to. For some people and cultures even, piercings and tattoos can be a healthy adornment and expression of their own personal style and self. However, for those who have numerous piercings, we may need to ask the questions: "Why do they want to suffer so many times? Why do they want to cover or transform their body?" The body is a natural house for life. So it could be said that drastic transformation of one's body through these procedures reflects an abandoned respect for their life. Of course, this is a personal choice for everyone that needs to be respected; however multiple tattoos and piercings could be a sign that something is wrong at a deeper level. Some are probably trying to fix something through the pain or embellishments. We could ask: "Why can't they accept themselves as they are?"

One observation I noted through different workshops and talking with people is that many teenagers who get piercings and tattoos in their self-discovery period, where they push their limits to find their true identity, want to remove them after a few years. Is this because they now feel free? Or do they understand something that they couldn't see clearly before?

In my understanding, once the piercings or tattoos are removed, a shift happens and they probably don't feel the need to subconsciously self-sabotage anymore. They now truly accept their human body.

Again, this is just a general observation worth investigating for certain people, in case this shows a predisposition towards suicide or another emotional issue that needs resolving. As tattoos and piercings are important, honored traditions for many cultures around the world, such as Buddhist monks in Thailand (tattoos), Massai tribe in Kenya (piercings) and lip plates in Ethiopia. Here, piercings and tattoos are an honored symbol of peoples' culture, beliefs and affiliations to their community and roots.

Anorexia can also be seen as a slow suicide. By not feeding themselves, people with the condition refuse the gift of life. Questions to ask: "Why are they following this slow, painful process towards death?" "Do they want to catch the attention of their parents?" "Is it a call for help?" Yes, most likely. Pay attention to the signs, ask questions and start the conversation. Don't turn a deaf ear or a blind eye to this disorder.

If a mother has had an abortion, she will sometimes want to follow her child and subconsciously die. Therefore one of her other children may unconsciously "take care of her" and want to die for her: "Dear Mom, I will die in your place." Bert Hellinger made this one of his key observations of Family Constellations. Always remember that a child is loyal to its parents and will do anything to release their pain.

Lastly, when a murder has not been recognized in the past, one member of the next generation might atone for her/his fate and commit suicide to bring order back into the family soul.

All of these examples have the same goal: "I will die in your place."

How can we release this family pressure?

With the help of Family Constellations, we can work with these invisible forces by rendering them visible in the light of the field. With this acknowledgment, these forces become conscious and the tension is released so everyone can see what is happening.

The family will start acting differently. It can be perceived as a spiritual act. A very powerful one!

Missing people need to be accepted, recognized and loved no matter what fate they chose to live. By respecting their fate, we respect the order in our system and it will release the heavy weight of secrets and accordingly, the unconscious desire to atone for someone or to balance the system through a suicide.

Everyone has a place in their family system. Everyone has the right to be part of a lineage. That's the gift of belonging.

Affirmations

You have a place in my heart. All of you.

In front of me, there is my life and I embrace it.

I respect your decision and bow to your fate, and I honor you as my father/mother (or other family member).

In-visible

If you feel an empty desire to follow your path, or are still clueless about why you feel bored and profoundly demotivated about your life, maybe it's time to start asking your family questions. They could know something that you were not aware of that feels like a missing piece.

Often the root of the problem lies in your lineage, not solely you.

Even if you do not get answers that seem to help, I would recommend that you create a little ceremony to recognize any missing people in your family.

You can write a letter, burn a candle or even plant a new tree or rose bush. Whatever new movement you initiate will trigger a shift that will contribute to a new beginning in your family nest.

"When you create a new flow of life, death [within the family system] will find peace." Marine Sélénée

Survival Instinct

Abuse. Sexual violence. Rape. Incest.

When we participate in a Family Constellations workshop, we might be confronted with these challenging issues and dynamics. We might even represent the perpetrator. I did. I represented an incestuous grandfather and I could feel his guilt, shame and inability to understand why he did it. Progressing into the field we then understood that he was a victim of his own grandfather as well. It did not mean that he had to be forgiven but at least acceptance was brought back into the field and he was able to say to his granddaughter through my voice, "I am sorry." It was a powerful resolution for their family but for me also regarding my past experience.

Often, the perpetrator is first a victim of another perpetrator, who was a victim of someone else and so on.

I am aware that it is a sensitive subject; however, I have met too many women who have been abused and just kept this destructive secret to themselves. As a result, some become very sexually active with no respect for themselves. Other women distance themselves from men, or become attracted to the same sex to feel safer.

In Family Constellations, we are not here to diminish this traumatic event, we are here to acknowledge this difficult experience and allow the client to accept it as it is, so that she or he is able to go and live her life fully, not just merely in survival mode.

Many women who I have spoken with on these issues remember the "before" and/or "after" phases distinctly; in the before moment they remember intuitively feeling danger and knowing that something was about to happen. In a way, they were prepared to live the worst. They couldn't concretely explain this feeling but for most, they already knew. This is why they had this willpower to generate a blackout to protect them. Some just got back to their lives without paying attention to this "accident" anymore. There was an urge, a survival instinct to get back to normal; a normal life avoiding what their body was trying to tell them.

The body and the mind do not forget these events. Sooner or later, the mind and body produce nightmares, flashbacks, visions and words to remember what happened. At this moment, women often turn to alcohol, drugs, and medication to numb the pain.

However, when the effects of the first dose or drink disappear, the only solution is to double the next intake and of course, by doing this, we can gradually enter a vicious circle where it is very difficult to get by and lead a full life.

We will never forget this kind of assault; it is imprinted in us. This event made us who we are, just as much as the good experiences we have had. It's a piece of us but it does not define us. The best way to deal with the event is to accept it as it is – an occurrence, nothing less and nothing more. Let's free ourselves from shame, guilt, and anger and allow us to see ourselves as strong women who, despite experiencing the worst, are not victims and will stand up keep going.

By standing up, our voice and commitment for our own life will protect future generations of women.

Affirmations

Healing myself is my priority.

This event does not define who I am. I am the one who defines me.

I won't let my scars make me a victim.

Forgiveness Versus Consenting

Many times I thought that by forgiving my perpetrator, I would feel better, more serene and at peace with what happened. I tried to forgive but I was never at peace. Actually, I was upset with myself for always playing the role of the strongest one who could handle anything. I did not want to be this person. I wanted to talk, understand and accept what happened.

My mind was an endless loop of racing thoughts. I felt only resentment and indigestion in my gut.

Regarding my abuse incident, forgiveness was hard for me to practice. At first, I tried exercises like "let it go", "send love to this person", and "see him as the little one he was", which helped me more than the absolute concept of forgiveness. However, I still felt trapped and uneasy at times, like I could not entirely digest the incident for good.

Finally, Family Constellations entered my life and I understood the power of consenting to 'what is' and then moving on from it. This was an epiphany for me.

You see, in Family Constellations, we don't forgive; we consent, accept and re-include. And this is how we can get such a deep, liberating healing. Because the thing with forgiveness is, there is an inequality. The one who starts the process of forgiveness will be seen as the bigger one and the other one as the little one. And, sooner or later, it won't bring anything good because of this unbalance.

In order to move forward, the situation has to find balance, a new harmony, a new center, and it does not happen with forgiveness but only with consent toward 'what is'. We know we cannot change the past, that's a fact, yet we are still addicted to our need to change the past. Are we stuck then? Only if we allow ourselves to be.

What can we do? Firstly, recognize what happened to you. To recognize means to listen. Listen to your pain, memories, and feelings. Create a healthy bond with it. Then, consent to what happened without trying to find the answer of "Why?" Don't fight anymore. It won't go anywhere. Surrender to what is. Release with love and acceptance and finally re-include this episode in its place in the past, where it belongs.

You cannot separate yourself from your dramas. The more you will resist, the more the dramas will be heavy to bear. When we accept our burdens, the associated heavy feelings are dropped instantly.

We cannot forgive the unforgivable but we can consent to it and make a statement that no matter what happened to us, tomorrow is another day, another chance. It's up to us to define ourselves and our days we want to live.

Consenting worked the best for me. I hope by reflecting on this idea of 'consenting to what is' will also help you in your own journey.

Who is Who?

Who is the victim? Who is the perpetrator? Who is feeding the bond between them? Who is challenging the other one to stay alive?

This dynamic between victim and perpetrator is very delicate and this is why I would like to write about it with respectful care. Even though I have personally experienced this dynamic, I need to respect the rights of other victims and perpetrators without judgment. Everyone has a different story and a unique way to handle it.

First, a perpetrator is only a victim of another perpetrator and so on. Until the perpetrator is acknowledged and given a place in the system, someone in a subsequent generation will become a perpetrator. It is important to note that despising the perpetrator fuels the perpetrator energy in the family system.

There must be peace for everyone, even the murderer, rapist or perpetrator. For this reason, it is crucial to recognize and give them a place in our family dynamic. Be informed that the perpetrator does not belong to it; he or she will only be recognized as they need to be. It's a form of deep respect for what is. It is an acceptance of our fate. In this approach, we will find peace.

For fifteen years, I fed the bond between my perpetrator and me. When I read about rapes or sexual abuse, I would shake. I was so upset; I wanted to kill all men. I wanted to destroy them just as one of them had destroyed me. I wanted revenge. Revenge for the young teenager I had been when it happened. Finally, I came to a place where I understood that my revenge was my condemnation. Through focusing on revenge, I condemned myself to never accept love again. It gave more power to my perpetrator, which was, of course, the opposite of my desire.

During my constellation, my facilitator placed the rapist out of my field and she added a scarf around him. This scarf represented his own field with his guilt. Plus, he turned his back from me. So I couldn't see his eyes. Respect was in my field and I felt safe to allow myself to finally drop this destructive anger that kept me from trusting men.

I felt empty and whole at the same time. I felt lighter. I was breathing deeper. I was alive. I was not challenging him anymore to be stand up and fight, to stay alive. I was free from him.

Despite the confronting nature of this constellation, it was a tremendous act of liberation.

I understood that I couldn't build something with revenge or anger. The only thing I could build was more anger, aggression and craziness. I didn't want to become a bitter person holding on to her pain as a right in order to survive. It does not define me. It's not my identity. It's a situation that happened a long time ago and in fact, it probably unveiled my true purpose.

Through processing my experience in Family Constellations and other methods - such as EMDR, yoga, guided meditation and the Law of Attraction teachings – I was able to deal with this event in a constructive, positive way. I decided to recreate something great from my terrible experience. Ultimately, this rekindled sense of positivity has given me the strength and courage to dream big and become the woman I am now.

When we face our shadows, they become smaller and then disappear. Living in our pain won't give us any prize. Let's release our pain, yes! The main prize is to achieve meaningful things that make us happy.

Happiness is an achievement of the soul. It's our choice. I don't minimize the effects of sexual abuse because for 15 years of my life, I struggled with its different effects. I know there is another way to acknowledge these effects and then move beyond the experience.

Let's release the shame from our story. We were innocent. Let's be proud of ourselves as women and men and stop self-sabotaging, because someone pretended our life was not important in one moment. This person couldn't even see us. He or she was only repeating something from his/her own field.

We are significant. We are more than a reflected image of our circumstance. We deserve to be happy and to be loved deeply and sincerely by our future or present partner.

Let's reconnect the love back into ourselves. Accept our past and be free from it.

My only role here is to tell us: it's worth it.

Affirmations

I am not my circumstances.

I am here and you are there.

I am free.

Letter to "Let-her" Be

I found one thing worked well in my healing process to help me let go of my abuse story.

It was to write a letter every week to myself.

My first few letters were very aggressive, violent and revengeful but finally through the process of writing, I was able to open my heart and understand that it was not my fault. I was not the guilty one and I should not be ashamed of it.

I recognized this event as it was. I discharged its impact and placed it where it belongs – in my past.

After a few weeks, I finally dropped this burden.

Who says that we have to rush?

Take your time with this task of resilience so you don't feel overwhelmed. It's a process – and a long one maybe – yet every 'letter-step' will always lead you to a more peaceful place than where you were before.

Toxic

How can we protect ourselves from toxic people, especially when they are from our family system?

First of all, sharing the same family system doesn't mean we have to share their toxicity. Blood does not create instinctive love. If we place ourselves and our life in the first position, our soul will be grateful.

It's challenging when we have to deal with poisonous people. It's even more challenging and hurtful when they are our mother, father or our sibling. If we adopt the role of victim, it will be perceived as revenge. No one can achieve a resolution with a revenge behavior. Everything comes from love. Our only option is to let go of any expectation of our parents. I know it might be shocking to read this but it is the truth.

Even though we could think of our father as absent or our mother as selfish, we have to let these perceptions go. We have our story and we are the writer of it, so please find other angles to describe them, especially our mother. I am sure we can find at least one good thing about her...because there's us, and she makes up half of us!

When we feel bad for our parents, we feel bad for ourselves. This is why healing is always about finding the right distance between ourselves and our parents. It's all about standing in our right place.

Forget about if we were desired or not at birth, as we are not able to know what really goes on inside another person. And these details are not significant. Since Bert

Hellinger has given birth to Family Constellations; we can take care of it and bring forth a wonderful and comforting resolution about our place in this world.

Complaining, blaming, and whining are toxic for our well-being. These defensive behaviors undermine our power. When we cut them out, we make the choice to grant ourselves a higher value and to stand up for our real self. Love is preceded by respect. When we respect ourselves, we will automatically bring love back.

This is exactly what happens during a constellation. We allow respect to enter the family dynamic so then love can enter. And so the miracle happens...

Affirmations

I choose to remove the toxicity from my life.

Nothing is personal.

I am surrounding myself with my Guardian field.

A Protective Field

Dealing with toxic energy is a part of life sometimes, unfortunately. The best way to protect ourselves and our mind from this is to mentally create a protective field. Name it and give it a color. As soon as we feel the need to be surrounded by guardian energy, call it!

Be a soldier of love. We don't fight darkness by sending more darkness; we fight by sending more love.

Color significance:

<u>White:</u> Purity, uncrossing, removing obstacles
<u>Grey:</u> Mental clarity, healing
<u>Red</u>: Passion, strength, physical energy
<u>Pink</u>: Love, self-love, affection
<u>Orange</u>: Success, encouragement
<u>Gold:</u> Glory, happiness, wishes
<u>Green</u>: Money, prosperity, luck
<u>Blue</u>: Peace, relaxation, tranquility
<u>Purple</u>: Power, ambition, finances
<u>Brown</u>: Being grounded
<u>Black</u>: Absorption of negativity
Yellow: Clarity, positivity, optimism

The Weight of Words:
A small talk may cause a big disaster

We have no idea how important and intense our words are and the repercussions they can have in our life. Our words represent what we think is 'right' and our truth.

What is the truth? How can we differentiate between a truth that is driven by our ego and a truth driven by our inner knowledge?

The truth today might not be the truth tomorrow. What's true when we are married, change when we are widowed. What's true when we are a young child, changes when we are an adult.

As our truth is in constant movement, our words, too. Every day, our truth changes because our life changes. It's an endless movement.

What's true for us might not be true for someone else. However, we have to honor and accept everyone's truth as long as this truth does not hurt ourselves.

Everyone has their own truth and sometimes, they don't want to hear another truth because they don't want to have to question themself.

You might not know what your loved ones are going through or what's truly happening inside them. So, please, don't make any assumptions regarding your truth because it only belongs to you, not to others, and be sure that when you want to speak your truth, it will come from a place of love. Only then, your truth can help instead of hurt someone. It takes guts to speak your truth. You could feel vulnerable because you may wonder if your truth will be welcome or not, but ultimately, you will be at peace with it by not trying to prove something to others.

This is why we think actions are better and more impactful than our words. This is why we may talk too much sometimes, when the best way to calm a situation down is to keep quiet.

We over talk issues. We cross the line and it becomes difficult to go back once we have. Sometimes it only takes one word.

As a matter of fact, we often won't remember the entire conversation, only specific words when the discussion became difficult.

I once wanted to resolve a dispute with a friend and we ended up fighting even more, exchanging words we wouldn't forget. Her words stuck with me for a long time.

From that time on, I always try to do my best when I have to confront someone, especially someone I love.

Our words are powerful. They have the power to destroy or uplift the other person. Let's pay attention to our words. With the rise of the Internet and social media, we often write without thinking about the impact of our words or their permanence. To stay out of drama, let's read over what we just wrote. Think before acting or posting. We can even send a draft to ourselves and then after several hours have passed, decide whether it is appropriate to send.

In Family Constellations, the weight of words is apparent. As facilitators, we have to choose words wisely when we work on a resolution. The best way is to find simple, concise words.

For example, it's always so powerful when an adult recognizes his father with the short statement: "Thank you for the gift of life. I am your son. You are my father."

It's a strong statement, a statement of love. Or when, someone says to a deceased family member who they are mourning or entangled with: "I will keep going on my life and I will see you when it is my time."

Let's keep our words simple and true. We will avoid many tears and misunderstandings. Let's talk with our heart. When we hesitate to talk to someone, accept this uncertainty and wait until tomorrow. We will probably have better words to express what needs to be said.

Lastly, our words represent our thoughts and consequently, ourselves. When we pay attention to our words, we pay attention to ourselves and therefore others.

Remember: our thoughts create our reality.

What reality do you want to live in?

What's the real truth? Authenticity. Truth is authentic power. We understand this once we are our whole, authentic selves.

Be authentic and pay attention to your words so they are always aligned with your true self.

Affirmations

I pay attention to my words -- I pay attention to my world.

My words become my thoughts. My thoughts become my actions.

As I give more meaning to my words, I give more love to my life.

Fluid Words

Pay special attention to your words. See where you can make more of an effort. Focus on the reactions of family, friends, and co-workers when you talk with them. Listen to the tone of your voice. Note when you feel aggressive and lose control of your words. Align with your own personal self-expression, it will reinforce the clarity of your thoughts and observations.

Money Motion

While money does not buy total happiness, it can contribute to it. Money can be our best or worst friend. Today, money might offer us a throne and crown; tomorrow, we might hit rock bottom.

In Family Constellations, financial issues are one of my clients' top concerns. Usually, they come to understand their financial loss or lack. The root of the issue is generally the same: the family has not recognized someone in the family system who died young or the family survived a painful event – war, famine, natural disaster and so on - and feels guilty about it.

By avoiding this recognition, we increase our chances of experiencing financial rollercoasters. We can be very wealthy for a few years and then experience a disastrous financial situation. We may reach out, succeed and then lose it all.

Feeling guilty on a deep level about our survival may compel us to create or attract situations in which we will be punished for living, especially living well. Punishment might come in the guise of losing our job, money or partner. Punishment may take form when we work under conditions that are unfair but we are afraid to stand up for ourselves.

For example, a few of my clients feel guilty and ashamed to have a job they like. So, unconsciously, they accept a lower income or work many hours, or do not take any time off. Often, this is so they can feed that unconscious loyalty toward their family. That pattern can comes from a severe incident in their family background, such as the Holocaust, slavery, and immigration caused by war, or violent and repressive dictatorship. Or, people who came from a wealthy family might not feel they are "enough" to take care of the inheritance, so they self-sabotage themselves.

To heal this situation, we need to recognize the deceased person or people and fall in love with our life and ourselves. Know deeply that we are enough and important, gives us an infinite value. Therefore there will be no shame regarding our skills, talents and how much we can make per year. This will free the family system and allow the prosperity flow to swing back into motion after it may have been interrupted for years.

Naturally, it is in our hands to nurture this new relationship with money. Once we heal the stagnant financial situation, we must then follow through and be consistent with the new dynamic. The healing will only last if we take care of it. Otherwise, the energized new flow we experience will disappear sooner or later.

Be aware that we don't own money. Money is a current, a flow. We must 'liberate' money, or it will find a way to escape our catch and imprisonment. Money goes where it is needed most, and stays when it is treated well. Our role is to reinvest and serve the world with our money to create a flowing motion. We give, we receive; it is a movement that joins us all together. We belong to the same community and world. We are together in this adventure.

So, let's be grateful for what we already have and we will attract more good things. Let's be respectful of our money. Be ready to receive it. Know that we deserve to get paid.

On top of that, let's be proud of our value. People who value themselves attract people who value them, too.

Remember that whatever we think about ourselves links directly to our feelings about money. Money is a reflection of how we see ourselves.

By honoring our money story, we honor our ancestors, our lineage and thus, the importance of our life. Let's create our own love affair with money and spread the Love!

Affirmations

I receive what I ask for.

Abundance is my birthright.

Money constantly flows into my life.

Abundance is a State of Being

The most important way to make money flow is to clear clutter!

Advice that has worked for me:

- Respect your wallet. Pay attention to it and clean it. Your wallet reflects how you treat your money. So if your wallet is in shreds or looking dirty and/or old, it's time to get another one! You could get a red or green one, which represent the colors of abundance in Feng Shui. Then, organize your wallet clearly and properly and clear out any clutter – such as unnecessary receipts, papers or business cards. Do this on a regular basis, so you can easily find your precious bills.

- Rename your saving or checking account as your 'abundance' or 'prosperity' account or even for one of your future projects or endeavors – for example, your wedding, a new car or a trip.

- When you pay a bill: Say "Thank you" and feel it deeply inside. You can even write it on your bill with a huge smiley face!

The Power of Dreams

'The interpretation of dreams is the royal road to knowledge of the unconscious activities of the mind. » Sigmund Freud

Our subconscious expresses itself through our dreams when we are sleeping. Quietly and peacefully, it sends us messages through our dreams. Sometimes, this could be through a nightmare but it always has a purpose.

Nightmares can be terrifying. They can stay with us for the rest of our day. Nightmares stay latent, underlying our thoughts before suddenly appearing as a vision in our sleeping brain. The furtive nature of nightmares can shock and destabilize us on waking, often leaving us clueless about their meanings.

Why does a specific nightmare consume our mind? What's the point? Where is the solution? Why is it recurring?

A recurring dream or a nightmare happens when we don't pay attention to its hidden messages. Nightmares are disguised, dramatized reflections of our own life story; existential questions regarding family and professional conflicts.

Dreams and nightmares help us to deal with our internal conflicts and regulate our emotions. They give us a chance to see a situation that looked foggy at first.

As my mom used to tell me when I was feeling uncertain or anxious about a situation: "After a good night's sleep, we will see clearer."

This is completely true! Our subconscious works for us! Our subconscious sends us new messages and signs through our dreams so that then when we wake, we can see the situation from a different angle.

When we sleep, we are so aware that we connect to our true self and thoughts; thoughts that can otherwise paralyze us during our conscious state, when other factors, such as ego, enter the equation. For example, we may have a strong intuitive urge to email a landlord about their place because we had a good feeling about it, however if we let our ego take over with self-sabotaging doubts or thoughts, we may not follow through and do anything. Yet, if you had a dream about this house and yourself in there, you will know your true feelings about this place. Or, you may see clues that you help you see if you can trust a particular person or if you should take a job offer that in the waking world, your ego may be pushing you to accept it or make a deal. But, through your dreams' metaphors, you will understand what your true self wants to do.

For this reason, I believe in prophetic dreams. We are involved with the non-physical world that is connected with the Universe. This world can show us the truth about situations and people.

We need to decode our dreams because the meaning is always beyond our first impression and perception. Go beyond the literal vision and story presented in our dreams; we need to dig deeper to know the real significance of the symbols, people and events featured. We have to analyze our present situation and make parallels with our dreams. We have to see the metaphor behind the rational.

A dream is another dimension; it can represent the big picture forest perspective, behind the narrow tree vision we see in our waking life.

If we understand our dreams, we will understand ourselves. We learn who and what surrounds us. We could even discover secrets from our family's past.

From a young age, I had a recurring dream that I finally understood at the age of 28. It's a very simple dream but a dramatic one. The setting is during a period of war or massacre, and I hide myself in a small room, cave or a secret place so no one can kill me. As soon as I don't hear any more noise, I go out of my hiding place and I become aware of being the only survivor. All of my family was killed. And then I wake up!

At 28, my mother told me a story about my paternal grandfather. When he was 13 years old, he had to hide out during World War II to escape capture and persecution by the Nazis. He changed his last name. Even though his family was not killed, in my subconscious I guess I am still connected there. So many others were killed; the ones who didn't had to hide to survive. Was I subconsciously carrying this weight, a heavy weight of a guilt that doesn't belong to me? This could be why my dreams sent me the message to heal this part of my heritage.

In a way my interrogation became real during one of my Family Constellations. I didn't constellate my dream; I constellated my guilt about wanting a beautiful, happy and abundant life. The field showed me that I was entangled with the guilt of a survivor. The survivor was my grandfather who I never met. But energetically and especially during my dreams, I could feel this palpable feeling of guilt.

Survivors bear a lot of guilt during the rest of their life, asking, "Why me and not the others?" This guilt could even drive them to insanity.

When we survive, we are not the hero. We are the lucky one. Because we think we need to atone for it, we transmit this feeling down through the generations. Yet, we don't need to keep these painful chains (or patterns) in our family. Suffering for something we didn't do or create doesn't serve us or them. Give the guilt back to the family member or the past where it belongs, and move on with profound respect and love.

Since I learned about this family story and came to terms with its significance, I've never had that nightmare again. I was able to stop hiding and come into the light, the light of my purpose.

Dreams can also mark the end of mourning. A few months after my grandmother passed away, she visited me in one of my dreams. It was so real; she was talking about everyone and their feelings during her funeral. At the end of her monologue, she told me that it was time for her to go and that I had to live my life in the now. I will never forget this dream. It was so deep and so true. I always had a beautiful connection with my grandmother and this dream topped it off.

Another dream I had involved meeting a palm reader in Key West and moving to New York. When I woke up, I wrote down the assignments presented in the dream.

Three days after, I was on the road for Key West. Six months after, I was on a flight for New York.

That might sound crazy to follow a dream but this one was very charged and I decided to trust it. Plus, my dreams have never betrayed me. I see them as an extension of my intuition. However, we have to act on them appropriately.

When there is a persistent dream, take a few minutes to recount it. Let the pen flow on the sheet of paper, writing down everything that pops into mind to describe it, so later on we can notice any particular signs.

We reach our maximum capacity when we are aware of all our gifts. By gift, I mean our body language, thoughts, dreams, afflictions and breath. We are a global entity, all united and connected to everything together. We are completely whole and aware.

Our dreams whisper to our conscious every night. They take their time because they don't want to frighten us; their aim is to show us something that needs to be unveiled. When the truth is recognized, we can give birth to a new flow in our life, our roots and our generation. It's a fresh impulse, offering us the chance to come closer to our true self.

Our dreams are the fastest way to reconnect with our true self and perceive things differently with more distance.

Dreams are one way to resolve a recurring situation. This is also the purpose of Family Constellations: to discover the truth and answers on our repetitive negative behaviors. It's a treasure hunt and the treasure is: knowing ourselves better.

Affirmations

My dreams have meaning. I pay attention to them.

I open my heart to receive important messages from my dreams.

Dear dreams, guide me to the truth.

Dream Diary

Before falling asleep, ask your dreams to give you answers about any situations or people about which or who you need guidance on. Maybe you won't get an answer the first night but sooner or later you will. So repeat your request every night until you get the answer. Write down all the details of your dreams that you can remember and wait. You don't have to think about it, if there is a meaning it will appear in your mind instantly. Have faith in your dreams.

Endless Movement

"When you accept the happiness that comes to you and again leaves, you accept also the gravity that is a part of life. And by welcoming in the sadness that comes through your door, you may find that in time it turns into happiness that stays with you. By opening the door to the sadness that comes to you, in time you may find that it is happiness that remains." Bert Hellinger

My grandfather, who is 82 years old, met another woman after he lost his wife three years ago. This may seem surprising for some people. For him, it is a perfect way to stay alive and enjoy the end of his life with someone. It's not about replacing my grandmother; it's only about love.

Who am I to judge him? Who am I to say it's wrong to be with another woman after more than 40 years of marriage to my grandmother who passed away? I am only his granddaughter and when my grandfather is happy, I am happy for him. Plus, I believe my grandmother is reassured that her husband is fine. Who knows, maybe wherever she is and with her new power (yes I love imagining my grandma as a powerful angel), she played the matchmaker.

The best part in life is to be open to opportunities and experiences. It is never too late to live a life we love. It is never too late to love again at any age.

I have clients who are 70 years old or more who want to work on their healing journey. They have this urge to put things in order and live life to the fullest. They are a great inspiration for me. They show me that life does not stop at any age and this lies in the power of the mind: when we internally or subconsciously say 'Stop', then life stops. And this can happen at any age.

The truth is we can die at any age. For this reason, release your hesitations to love, enjoy, say "yes", take risks, follow your passions and listen to your heart more. You get my point! Be a little 'more'. Live each day like your last and I guarantee your life will be more than fun!

Love is a movement. Hate is roadblock. With love we will always evolve. With hate we will always stay in our uncomfortable, grumpy zone. Love is wide, hate is narrow.

A person who doesn't love is afraid of love. When one loves truly, one forgets fear. It's like being on a diving board: those on the platform are afraid but others are not.

So jump! Create a movement!

When we look at our fears, we make them smaller. Through the action of acknowledgement, we will leave them behind. Fears only exist because we let ourselves be guided by them and run away from them. As soon as we recognize our fears, we shift the focus and they fade away!

Replace this sense of fear with the sense of love. We will see how our life makes a tremendous shift.

Love is connected with hopefulness, joyfulness, greatness, boundlessness, gratefulness, happiness and so on. With love, we can achieve anything.

By creating a movement of love in our life, we create a better vibration within ourselves; therefore we will attract good opportunities and encounters.

In Family Constellations, we move things from the hidden part of the mind to the open through language. When things are explicit they can be used in favor of the client. When the client can express his true feelings about any member of his family or his experiences, love will return. When love returns we find resolution. Again, Family Constellations are about love, nothing else.

It's the lack of love that creates depression, anger, fear, doubt, aggression, inconsistence, cruelty, grief, pain, victimization, misunderstandings, murder and disease.

So...

If our grandfather wants to love again, encourage him!

If we want to embrace our true passion, embrace it!
If we want love, spread it!
If we want to be a soldier of love, be an example!

The opposite of love is hate. In my mind, indifference is a more brutal response. With hate, we still keep feeling something. With indifference, we just sink into a state of numbness.

I would say that with hate, there is still the belief that tomorrow will be better. With indifference, the question is closed.

Nothing lasts and everything is solvable. As soon as our perception is aligned with love and being for and not against, we will be grounded with our true self, that is – Love.

Affirmations

I am love.

I choose love.

I love Love.

'Love' Vision

Create a vision statement.

Ask yourself: "What would my life be like if I knew I was always being guided by love?"

Surrender to your boldest creative thoughts and imagine what life would be like if you knew you were always being guided. If you feel even the slightest sense of peace after reading your vision statement, then you are tapping into your truth.

What are you waiting for to experience the life you just described?

Let 'Love' be your guide.

Healing: where you arrive is where it begins

After experiencing a resolution in the field, we always feel high. We finally understand many aspects and it feels empowering and magical. Our first thought could be « Wahoo, I am healed! » In a way, it's true. However, we need to keep our guard up. This lightness and feel good sensation generally only last for a few weeks. When the resolution is completely integrated internally, the orgasmic feeling disappears. We may retain the happiness but not the magic. When we become addicted to that enlightenment and resist going back to a normal state, do we know what that means? It means we are probably more concerned about feeling high than healed.

A heroin addict knows heroin isn't good for their health; however the thrilling, fulfilling feelings they get from a hit is so good that they don't think about the next day or consequences, death included.

To heal, we must overcome our addiction to being high. To be high, we need to suffer and if we heal, we won't suffer anymore. It's a vicious circle to monitor carefully.

This is why we need to be committed to our healing. It is the most important aspect of growth. Without our commitment, our helpers' dedication will be useless. We have to work continuously and not look for rainbows and butterflies.

The goal of therapy or healing techniques is not to cover the pain by getting a 'hit' from 'aha' moment resolutions; it's to reveal the pain, acknowledge it, accept it and move forward. Happiness is an achievement of the soul. It's not a superficial, quick fix deal. It's an endless state. We have to be super realistic in our healing journey and approach it from a mindful, adult perspective. We have to be aware that happiness takes time, it won't happen in a day and we must be willing to commit to it for the rest of our life.

We need to practice "happiness" every day. This will be the difference between where we are standing right now and where we want to go.

We feel good because we want to feel good. We find a way to align with what we want to feel good. This is the real life experience.

Let's open our eyes to beauty. Focus on joy. Think of positive things. Follow the impulse to be happy.

Let's be aware of where we are vibrationally. Then, let's speak our truth.

Engagement, commitment and practice are the three invaluable keys for deep healing. Love surrounds these keys above all.

It's easy to love ourselves when everything flows. The devotion to our goal of happiness will be harder when things arise to challenge us. When those days come, see them as training, and above all let's love ourselves more.

One of my favorite quotes:

Our deepest fear is not that we are inadequate. Our deepest fear is that we are powerful beyond measure. It is our light not our darkness that most frightens us. We must ask ourselves, who am I to be brilliant, gorgeous, talented and fabulous? Actually, who are you not to be? You are a child of God. You playing small doesn't serve the world. There is nothing enlightened about shrinking so that other people will not feel insecure around you.

We are born to make manifest the glory of God that is within us. It is not in just some of us; it's in everyone. And as we let our own light shine, we unconsciously give people permission to do the same. As we are liberated from our own fear, our presence automatically liberates others.

Marianne Williamson

Affirmations

I am worthy of happiness.

I choose what makes me happy today.

My vulnerability is my true strength.

Sparkling Slivers

A healing journey is a process. It can't happen in one day. You have to be consistent and committed to your healing. Some days, you will want to give up. During those days when your energy is down, think about why you started your journey. Why did you make the choice to become a better version of yourself every day? Happiness is only a perception, and this is why you have to nurture the perception every day with small things. Pay attention to the little things each day– a smile from a stranger, a cupcake, a sunray on your balcony – these are messages of love. Notice and be thankful for them.

Be grateful and thankful for the beauty in your life. Every morning or night, write down 10 things that you are grateful for. Do this for at least 40 consecutive days. By paying attention to your blessings, you will reinforce your healing journey.

Harmony

When the family system is in order, there is a feeling of relief and peace. All of our life experiences start working harmoniously together again.

Every time I receive a new resolution, it is always a meaningful moment.

A year ago, I experienced a beautiful resolution that will always keep an important place in my heart.

The night before the resolution, I had an ocular migraine, which caused blurred vision and a headache. I went to bed and slept for 12 hours!

When I arrived at the workshop, the first thing I heard was a woman who was participating to the workshop, talking about the significance of the eyes: "...the soul of the father is in the right eye and the mother's is the left..."

At that moment, I knew this journey was going to be special.

We were in a circle and one by one, we described the issue we wanted to work on. When it was one man's turn, I looked at him for the first time. I hadn't seen or noticed him until then. I could only see his profile. However, suddenly he caught my attention. There was something about him that was very disconcerting for me.

I realized he bore an uncanny resemblance to my father. I was hypnotized. He wore the same glasses, jeans, and luxury shoes. He had the same grey hair, height and made the same gesture of touching his stomach. Maybe I was trying to convince myself that there was a part of my father in him but no! I spent six hours with this man and I guarantee that I was not insane or wishful; I was not trying to see my father in him. I seized this chance to speak with my father through this man in silence.

When he stood up to represent someone in the field, I was swamped by a huge wave of emotions. I started talking to my inner father, silently within. I used this man to finally have my talk with him. Several times, tears came to my eyes.

During the entire day, I kept him in my field of vision. I was gripped by this sign I believe my angels gave me. Truthfully, I wasn't present in the circle. I felt selfish in this workshop. I just wanted to speak to my father through this man. However, sometimes that's how we are able to give – by first taking care of our needs in a real, open way.

At the end of the day, I went over to this man to get his business card. He gave me his card and here was the final touch. His name was William, the same as my brother. I was so shocked that he asked me if there was something wrong with his name. I told him the truth about my resolution. He just hugged me and I whispered, "Thank you."

Thank you William, for representing my father in silence, exactly how he is.

This was a harmonious day that added a new note to the sheet music that my dad and I have shared since my birth, whether he is present or not.

Affirmations

In every situation, I see a means to resolve one of my shadows.

Resolutions bring me peace.

I open my mind and my heart to receive guidance that will lead me to a resolution.

Sheet Music

It is always trickier to make peace with someone who is still alive and doesn't want to see you, or, when the lines of communication are down in a particular relationship. First, you need to accept the decision, then you will be able to send love.

To help you in this process, create a list of a family members or significant others you are/feel estranged from or are having difficulty communicating with. Note all of the things you are grateful to him or her for. Write down all the good memories of this person. See the good in this person. If it's your mother or father, at the very least, they gave you everything – life!

Every time you experience a moment of doubt, read your gratitude list about this person and you will see your energy rise quickly!

Small Miracles and Moments of Grace

I have experienced many insights into family system dynamics since I became involved in Family Constellations. Every time, I have been amazed to see what appeared in the field. I would like to share a few of these stories to illustrate the power of this healing modality.

1) A woman had five abortions. She was clueless about her behavior. She didn't know why she was repeating the same issue, even though she wanted to have a baby one day. The field revealed to her that she was loyal to her mother. Indeed, her mother has six kids. The client was the youngest one. The mom tried to abort the first five children without success. When she got pregnant with her last daughter however, she decided to follow through with the pregnancy without entertaining any thoughts of abortion. However, the youngest daughter always heard her talking about her five unsuccessful abortions. When the client got the resolution, her face became radiant. In bringing everything to awareness she could understand herself, take responsibility, love herself, and begin to imagine moving on.

2) A woman was desperate to attract her soul mate. She didn't understand why she was so attracted to 'bad guys'. When the facilitator set up her constellation, the client just ran away from the person representing her soul mate. She would have actually left the room she was that scared of him and his love for her. She was scared to suffer again. She was just not ready for him. When she saw this

dynamic she understood that it was not men s' fault, rather, she needed to heal herself first. This was a huge relief for her." As Bert Hellinger says, "The wrong way is endless."

3) A gay man lost his dad when he was seven years old. Everyone in his family often told him that his dad would never have accepted his sexuality. He felt very guilty about it. The field revealed that his dad was already aware of his son's sexuality and he wasn't upset by it, at all. It was a huge breakthrough for the client. He was finally able to accept himself entirely without any guilt.

4) A woman always thought that she had an older brother. She wanted to know if the field would show this dynamic. It did. According to the field, her father had a first child and he was likely an unborn baby or a miscarriage. She got her resolution and a few weeks later during a family dinner, her dad told the family that before he met his wife, he had a relationship with someone else. He left her without knowing that she was pregnant. She had a baby, a son, who unfortunately died after six months.

These few examples alone illustrate the power we can experience through a Family Constellation. When I participate in Family Constellations, I am always speechless. Every time, I get a different resolution about an issue that allows me to be more present in my life. I have felt grounded ever since I discovered Family Constellations.

I loved the exploration into my roots and who I am. The process of putting my family puzzle pieces together transformed from hidden alleys of fear initially into a fascinating journey. Try it!

Affirmations

I celebrate synchronistic moments when the mysterious flow of life brings me to the right place, at the right time.

I come to understand that I am being guided by an invisible hand. Trusting this, I rest in the perfection of each moment.

The Universe has my back.

Imitation

What about you? Can you make any connections between your actual behavior and the behaviors of your ancestors? Are you unwittingly imitating someone in your family? Or do you repeat the same behavior without having any clues as to why?

If you made your family tree in the first chapter, take another look at it and see if you can make any connections between one destiny and another. Let your intuition guide you into the labyrinth of your roots.

Surrender

When was the last time we surrendered entirely to ourselves? When did we simply trust the flow of our path, without knowing anything about where the path was heading?

This means experiencing life without a safety net and having faith in our day. Letting things run their course, without doubt.

When did we last surrender? If we can't remember, it's time to bring trust back into our life. When we trust, we have faith to surrender all of our fears, doubts and worries.

By letting the Universe (or the entity that is meaningful to us) guide us with signs, messages and whispers from our inner voice, we completely appreciate being alive. We will see things differently. We will be satisfied with particular or casual situations. Our breath will become deeper and more grounded. We will feel rooted and fully present. We will be able to experience the power of now that could give us spectacular shifts for our healing and spiritual journey.

This ultimate surrender can be seen as an epiphany. In this clarity, we will acknowledge our true self and the power of our thoughts will be unlimited. We will make great choices for ourselves and automatically, this beautifully impacts our environment and people who surround us everyday

By letting go, we allow others to do the same. We create a movement. This movement is a wave of love, trust and serenity. We will savor bliss even during challenges, because we know how to overcome our shadows and fears. We will be surrounded by a light that guides our way.

Our body and aura will radiate confidence and love, thereby attracting great opportunities and encounters, further feeding our happiness.

With this feeling of empowerment, we may release and surrender, disconnecting from people who no longer serve us. We will see more clearly who is here for us and who is not. Habits that are no longer useful will be released too.

We will be entirely involved in every moment of our life. We will make love with passion and devotion to our lover. We will give without expectation of others. We will receive without any guilt. We will embrace our meaning without any shame. We will look people in the eyes. We will speak our truth. We will follow our desire. We will dream bigger and bigger because we will know that we are unlimited.

If we want to experience this feeling of unlimited power, Family Constellations can help us to achieve our quest.

When we enter into the field and start constellating our family system --or any issue that we have to deal with-- the authentic truth that emerges can free us from old tethers. This understanding will allow us to release the string so that we can accept and love ourselves. This is the breakthrough, through invisible walls without the need to change our story.

Family Constellations can guide us in our healing venture. This philosophy gives us permission to be fully aligned with our emotions and feelings about events and people. Only love is present in the field. There is no place for judgment, accusation, violence or rejection. Those old ways are what caused troubled dynamics in the first place. Everyone will be recognized and loved. We will make peace with our past and the effects on our present shall be tremendous!

When will we understand that our power lies in our surrendering mindset? When will we accept to just be? When will we understand that surrendering is the start? The start of freedom, the start of happiness, the start of joy and so many more amazing things! Surrender and then you will be in full power. Controlling is only resistance and we are never powerful when we are resistant to life. We are tired, frustrated, angry, depressed and don't look at being happy!

When we surrender, we get the answers that, we were looking for.

So, repeat after me: "I surrender to the power that is mine."

Just be. Be in the now. You're seen, you're heard and, yes, you belong to us. You can be vulnerable because your real strength is there. You can be who you are. So, please, surrender to your true self.

Affirmations

I will slowly let go of the people who no longer serve my life and who I can no longer serve.

I am surrendering.

I am in the now.

Start Anew

Imagine that you have the capacity to surrender whatever is blocking your way, right now. This new approach to your life gives you a fresh aura and power. You are indestructible. You can attract everything you want.

What will you dare to do? Which new resolutions will you make? What will your next actions be?

See yourself filled with capacity and dream big!

In your notebook, write down your answers to the above questions, so step by step, you can start creating the life of your dreams,

You are capable. You are enough. Spread your wings.

Commitment

Here we are in the last chapter, number 33, symbolizing the last vertebra.

We have been working on our spinal cord throughout this book and it is almost in 'movement'. Hopefully our back will already feel stronger and our feet more grounded. Even if we haven't done all the exercises or affirmations so far, we can commit to this maxim: "Today is the first day of the rest our life."

Today is a new chapter, a new beginning. I want us to commit to ourselves. I like the way the word commitment sounds like 'come meet me', an apt description for the commitment and compromise needed to reach your true self.

I want us to take what resonated personally for us through reading this book and leave the rest. The most important thing is to be in movement. Movement in our decisions, actions, thoughts, words. In movement, we can avoid a lot of useless thoughts or behaviors. By being in continuous movement, our mind will focus on the essential tasks and steps required to keep moving forward.

As soon as we feel stuck: let's Dance, Move, Laugh, Run, Walk, Make Love, Sing, or Write...

Let's create a wave of hope and revive our energy.

In action, we feel courage over fear. We feel discovery over loss. We feel love over hate. We feel willpower over despair. We feel support over rejection. We feel the present moment over the past and future. We feel alive over being sick.

The fear of change blocks us from embracing our life's honesty and our incredible power! "What if?" is a phrase that could be banished from our mind! Something will happen but why focus on the worst case scenario instead of the best? What's the point? Where is the pleasure in imagining burdens and sufferings that don't even exist yet?

As my teacher, Michelle said: "A happy ending cannot happen in the middle of the story." So, live the story – wake up, breathe and make the choice to be happy every day.

Today, I choose to be … happy, abundant, fierce, prosperous, funny (pick your words!)

Dare to have the life that you want and fall fearlessly in love with it.

In this new beginning, dare to be YOU.

Affirmations

I will live my life to the fullest today

I will start to let go of the things that are not serving me well.

I will embrace my new beginning.

"Come Meet Me"

Experience a Family Constellations session!

Please refer to the list in the appendix for resources on finding a facilitator in your area.

Acknowledgements

After three years, I finally have the book that I wanted to read when I was starting my journey.

It's a part of me, my family, love life, experiences and so much more. Thank you to all of you who contributed to it. You were my teachers; you helped me to become this woman that I wanted to be. The polishing is still in process but I can proudly say without a doubt that I finally love it!

Thank you to all of my angels who had a tiny or huge impact in my life - without you it wouldn't have been the same.

My love especially goes to my....

Parents. You were and are still amazing. I love you so much.
Brother. I love you.
Little girl. We are doing a great job! I love you.
Grandparents. Thank you for your love, patience and teachings. Mame, one day, I will teach my children, how to talk to roses...
Godson. Thank you for your love and being unique. Never let anyone tell you what you are capable of because you can achieve whatever you want. I love you.

To my family and cousins, especially Nono. I will always remember our conversations that make me smile.

To my friends...I am so grateful to have so many good, talented and fascinating friends. Thank you for your support, laughs, tears, love, confidences, strengths and so much more. You are my treasures. Anne-Cecile, Laetitia, Deborah, Celine, Leslie, Cecilia, Elodie, Marie, Isabelle, Christelle, Michele, Alison, Denise, Medhi, Romain, Antoine, Baptiste, Claire, Priscilla, Amy, Marietou, Jessica, Jennifer, Erika, Delphine, Alexia, Dan, Laurence, Come, Eva, Veronique, Lydie, Marion, Ellen, Gaelle and Jenny.

To my teachers and healers...Emmanuelle, Michelle, Mariola, Phillia, John, Stuart, Amanda, Nina, Sabine, Mimi, Johanna, Nikki, Danielle, Kenny, Suzi, Natalie, Georgette, Erika and Ruby.

To my lovers and to you my love, who makes every new day spent with you magical.

To Maha Rose and Awakening in Greenpoint, Brooklyn; the first healing centers that believed in me. Thank you for your trust.

To RKA Ink Team. Thank you for your amazing work on my website and book cover. You rock!

Finally, I thank all of my clients who have shared their stories and opened their hearts with me over the years. It's been a complete honor, with many astonishing moments. I bow to each and every one of you.

References / Bibliography

Page 13: Toni Morrison. (n.d.). BrainyQuote.com. Retrieved November 17, 2015, from Brainyquote.com
Website :
http://www.brainyquote.com/quotes/quotes/t/tonimorris161280.html

Page 23: Marianne Williamson, 2004, *The Gift of Change*, Harper Collins Publisher, New York, NY

Page 35: Bert Hellinger, 2001, *Love's Own Truths*, Zeig, Tucker & Theisen, Inc, Phoenix, AZ

Page 38: Bert Hellinger, 2001, *Love's Own Truths*, Zeig, Tucker & Theisen, Inc, Phoenix, AZ

Page 41: Daniel Booth Cohen, *Messengers of Healing: The Family Constellations of Bert Hellinger Through the Eyes of a New Generation of Practitioners*, Zeig, Tucker & Theisen, Inc and J. Edward Lynch, Phoenix, AZ

Page 59: Bert Hellinger, 2001, *Love's Own Truths*, Zeig, Tucker & Theisen, Inc, Phoenix, AZ

Page 64: Jodi Picoult, 2009, *Handle With Care: A Novel*, Atria Books, New York, NY

Page 86: Suicide 2015. In the Free Dictionary by Farlex, *Dictionary* online.
Retrieved from :
http://www.thefreedictionary.com/Kill+yourself

Page 109: Bert Hellinger, 1998, *Love's Hidden Symmetry: What Makes Love Work in Relationships*, Zeig, Tucker & Theisen, Inc, Phoenix, AZ

Page 112: Marianne Williamson, 1992, *A Return to Love*, Harper Collins Publisher, New York, NY

Resources and Extra Support

EMDR

Francine Shapiro, 2001, *Eye Movement Desensitization and Reprocessing (EMDR): Basic Principles, Protocols, and Procedures*, The Guilford Press, New York

Francine Shapiro, 2012, *Getting Past Your Past: Take Control of Your Life With Self-Help Techniques From EMDR Therapy*, Rodale, New York

Family Constellations

Joy Manne, 2009, *Family Constellations: A Practical Guide to Uncovering the Origins of Family Conflict*, North Atlantic Books, California

Bert Hellinger, 1998, *Love's Hidden Symmetry: What Makes Love Work in Relationships*, Zeig, Tucker & Theisen, Inc, Phoenix, AZ

Bert Hellinger, 2001, *Love's Own Truths*, Zeig, Tucker & Theisen, Inc, Phoenix, AZ

Bert Hellinger, 2014, *Looking Into the Souls of Children*, Hellinger Publications, Germany

Find a facilitator

New York State:

> Marine Sélénée
> Marineselenee.com

Suzi Tucker
Suzitucker.com

Natalie Berthold
Natalieberthold.com

California:

Mark Wolynn
http://www.markwolynn.com

Miami:

Michelle Blechner
Themissinglinkbymichelleblechner.com

John Moore
Peacethroughoneness.com

Family Constellations Therapy US:

http://www.hellingerpa.com

http://familyconstellations-usa.com

Bert Hellinger – Founder of Family Constellations

http://www2.hellinger.com

Eating Disorders

National Eating Disorder Association – www.neda.org (to find a specialist / therapist in your area)

The books that made a difference for me...

Psychomagic by Alejandro Jodorowsky

The Zahir by Paolo Coelho

May Cause Miracles by Gabrielle Bernstein

The Four Agreements by Don Miguel Ruiz

Reconciliation by Thich Nhat Hanh

Essential Ayurveda by Shubhra Krishan

The Instinct to Heal by David Servan-Schreiber

And Never Stop Dancing by Gordon Livington

The Secret by Rhonda Byrne

The Why Café by John P. Strelecky

You Can Heal Your Life by Louise Hay

The 8 Human Talents by Gurmukh

A Return to Love by Marianne Williamson

The Man Who Wanted to be Happy by Laurent Gounelle

Wild by Cheryl Strayed

Les Lumieres de l'Invisible by Patricia Darre (French)

About the Author

Marine Sélénée is the creator of Marine Sélénée The Movement - an inspirational approach to life and holistic healing service, through marineselenee.com, her dedicated online resource; personalized coaching programs, Family Constellations, Organizational workshops and The Happiness Movement (In-person happiness Labs and other fun enlightening workshops).

As an integrative coach, Family Constellations facilitator, Reiki practitioner and motivational speaker she helps and guides her clients to a point where they can fly on their own.

Her approach is simple: create a life of fulfillment, a life that is constantly moving in the direction of pure joy, empowerment and accomplishment.

Her background in communications and psychology, as well as her own challenges thinking she was "not-enough" led her to develop her own tools and tips that form part of her own business you see today at marineselenee.com and in her practice. She unlocked, released and healed all the patterns and burdens that were blocking her path to become the happy girl that she was meant to be.

Her energy, passion and dedication to her beliefs in healing and empowerment is infectious.

29032697R00106